The Hostess Book of
ENTERTAINING

The Hostess Book of
ENTERTAINING

Marguerite Patten

DAVID & CHARLES
Newton Abbot London North Pomfret (Vt)

(Frontispiece)
Traditional Christmas
Dinner — Smoked Salmon
Cornets, Roast Turkey with
Bread and Cranberry Sauce,
Christmas Pudding and
Mince Pies in a Hostess
Console trolley (see page 51)

Acknowledgements
The colour pictures are reproduced by
courtesy of the following: White Fish
Kitchen, pages 11, 76 and 113; British
Turkey Federation, British Poultry Meat
Association and H.P. Bulmer Ltd, page 15;
Carmel Products Information Bureau pages
23 (above) and 60; Flowers and Plants
Council, page 23 (below); John West, pages
27, 30, 65 and 101 (above); Taunton Cider,
page 35; The Danish Centre, pages 49 and 81;
Lea and Perrins, page 57; British Turkey
Federation, page 72; New Zealand Lamb
Information Bureau, 80 and 85; British
Duck Advisory Bureau, page 88; Billingtons
Natural Brown Sugars, page 101 (below);
Flour Advisory Bureau, pages 108 and 117
The remaining pictures on pages 2, 19, 34,
41, 44, 53, 93, 97 and 121 were specially
commissioned for this book by Ekco Heating
& Appliances.

Patten, Marguerite
    The Hostess book of entertaining.
1. Entertaining
I. Title
642'.41   TX731

ISBN 0-7153-8049-4

Library of Congress Catalog Card Number
80-67394
©Ekco Heating & Appliances 1980

Printed in The Netherlands
by Smeets Offset BV, Weert
for David & Charles (Publishers) Limited
Brunel House Newton Abbot Devon

Published in the United States of America
by David & Charles Inc
North Pomfret Vermont 05053 USA

Contents

Introduction

Many factors contribute to a perfect party or special celebration, including good food, attractive table settings and flowers, compatible guests, but above all else, a relaxed and confident hostess.

The purpose of this book is to cover all aspects of entertaining and so help each busy hostess to look forward to the party without worrying or having misgivings.

I have given a selection of menus to suit most tastes, budgets and occasions, together with information on shopping for the food, hints on making cooking as easy as possible, and suggestions for presenting the dishes and keeping the food hot or cold and in perfect condition until ready to serve.

Entertaining at home enables you to plan exactly the kind of menu you feel each guest will enjoy, often selecting less usual foods and cooking more interesting dishes than those available in a restaurant. Even if you choose very luxurious foods for your menu it will prove considerably cheaper to prepare the dishes at home, rather than purchasing a comparable meal in a restaurant. In these days, when many households have a freezer as well as a refrigerator, you will find much of the preparation of the meal can be carried out in advance, and information on freezing ahead is given under each recipe where this is applicable.

Good food is only one aspect of good entertaining; in other sections of the book are suggestions for table settings, flower arrangements and general hints on making your guests feel welcome. This is another advantage of home entertaining; you can provide a much more free-and-easy and leisurely atmosphere than you would expect to find even in a first-class catering establishment.

Obviously, no-one anticipates failures or mishaps with any degree of pleasure, but if something goes amiss in the kitchen, or an accident happens such as wine being spilt on a pale carpet, it is often relatively simple to rectify this if you follow the correct procedure. I have, therefore, included some information on this subject.

The purpose of this book is to simplify entertaining, and to make the occasion memorable and enjoyable for the hostess, host and the guests.

Marguerite Patten.

1 Ways to Entertain

Do not imagine that every form of party-giving must entail a great deal of work and/or expense. These are various ways of entertaining your friends and acquaintances, some more elaborate than others:

A Coffee Party
Coffee mornings are a popular means of raising money for charity, but a private coffee party can be a very pleasant and relaxed occasion. There is little work to do and the cost of the food is relatively small. If you have a large number of guests and limited coffee-making facilities you may need to prepare some coffee ahead. See pages 122 and 123.

A Luncheon Party
It is traditional, although not essential, for a luncheon menu to be lighter and less elaborate than the meal served for an evening dinner party. This book also has two low-calorie menus; these would be ideal for a ladies' luncheon where the guests are watching their weight. On a hot day you could serve the meal on the patio or in the garden. Dishes suitable for outdoor eating are included in Chapter 5.

A Tea Party
British teas have been famous for decades and many visitors to this country would be disappointed if they missed a really interesting afternoon tea, although the sandwiches, cakes, and other foods are surprisingly sustaining.

A Cocktail Party
This name is still given to a drinks party although nowadays most people seem to prefer more straightforward drinks. It is a good way of entertaining a relatively large number of people.

A One-Dish Party
One of the most familiar versions of this party is to serve cheese with wine. Some classic recipes would form a good basis for a one-dish party. See pages 110 to 116.

A Dinner Party
This allows one to spend time with a relatively small number of people and so enjoy their company to the full. There is no one ideal dinner party menu but there are certain 'golden rules' about selecting the dishes to achieve an outstanding meal. See Chapter 5.

A Buffet Party
There is something pleasantly informal about serving this kind of meal; most guests will enjoy helping themselves to the food and it gives the hostess a chance to entertain a greater number of people at one time.

What They Entail

A Coffee Party
Really good coffee (kept hot or iced). Serve biscuits, cake or gâteau, or piping hot scones. Recipes are on pages 118 to 120.

A Luncheon Party
If the luncheon party is for ladies, the dishes should look rather pretty and feminine. If children are among the guests adapt more sophisticated food. See page 52.

Tea Party
This will vary according to the season. In winter serve hot buttered crumpets or fingers of toast. In summer use soft fruits as a filling and topping for a sponge.
Traditional British tea menus are given on pages 117 and 118.

A Cocktail Party
A selection of drinks and finger-sized savouries. Recipes are on pages 31, 56 and 58.

A One-Dish Party
An excellent choice of cheese and wines. A single dish must be outstanding in flavour.

A Dinner Party
A careful choice of menu, to give a good balance of flavour, texture and colour, with the wines that complement the food.

A Buffet Party
Imaginative dishes (many buffet party menus are dull) and food that is easily served and simple to eat with a fork.

2 Planning Ahead

A Visitors' Book

A visitors' book should not only be a record of people who have visited your home and have been entertained by you, but should be a practical book of reference. It will be of great value in giving you a well-justified reputation as a considerate hostess. The book can list:

The menus you serve, so that you can be sure you do not repeat the same dishes for your guests, unless by special request.

The individual likes and dislikes (if any) of your guests. Special dietary needs if your guests are of a particular religion or have to follow a set pattern of eating, eg they could be strict vegetarians, have to follow a fat-free diet, or be allergic to shellfish etc. It is much easier to know about these facts before your guests arrive and make suitable preparations ahead.

You may also like to record any special interests of the guests; this makes it easier to start a conversation and enables you to add a brief sentence about their hobbies when introducing people to one another.

It may seem strange to compare formal entertaining with a military operation, but there are certain similarities. In both cases it is advisable to plan ahead if you want everything to run smoothly, and yet be so flexible that if something goes wrong you can successfully change, or adapt, your original ideas.

The kind of pre-planning that makes entertaining run smoothly and become less hard work is as follows:
1 Select your guests; then plan the kind of food and drink that would please *them* and fit within your household budget.
2 Write a comprehensive shopping list, working out the foods and drinks that can be purchased well ahead and those that need to be bought at the last minute; obviously, this list will depend upon whether you intend to cook certain dishes well ahead and put them into the freezer.
3 Write another list, this time to cover the jobs, apart from cooking, that will need to be done, such as arranging the flowers, polishing the silver; either chilling the white wine or opening the red wine in plenty of time so that it may breathe.
4 Work out the order of the preparation and cooking of the food to ensure that everything is ready at the right time. This is less important if you have an efficient means of keeping the cooked food hot (see pages 40 to 47). Remember to include in this list the defrosting and reheating of foods and prepared dishes from your freezer. Do put your lists in a safe place so they are readily available, as and when required.

Your Guests

Your choice of guests will play an important part in the success of any special occasion, so select these with due thought. Whilst it may seem a wise idea to invite a group of people who all have the same interests, the conversation and atmosphere can be more lively and stimulating if you deliberately introduce a new element into an already established group of friends. It is, however, considerate to plan your guest list so that you are sure each person will find at least one 'soul-mate'.

The number of guests you invite will vary a great deal. In the case of a dinner party you will find some menus in this book which are planned for a minimum of six people, others for eight; this assumes there are the host and hostess or just a host or a hostess, and four, or six, guests. Obviously there will be times when you have more people to a meal but six or eight always seems an ideal number for a dinner party.

The paragraph above is only a general observation. If you live alone you may just want to invite one guest and you will find several pages of recipes which are suitable for dinner for two. It is quite wrong to assume that you must have an even number of guests. Sometimes a person who has recently lost a husband or wife finds that they are not asked out as often as they might be, as they are just one person. You can always arrange a table so that one person fits in quite easily and you could have seven, instead of eight, people. If inviting a single person, it might be sensible to invite a guest of the same, or other, sex, who would in effect be their partner at the dinner table, although the formal days of each person having to have a partner are, thankfully, over.

Modern homes often have a small dining room and if you try and crowd too many people round the table there are difficulties in seating and in serving the meal. One must also think most carefully about the seating arrangements in the sitting room before and after dinner.

To invite two guests only can be delightful, if they are parents, children, or close friends, or if business is to be discussed at the meal; it does, however, place a considerable burden on the host and hostess, who have to keep the conversation going, as well as look after the welfare of the guests.

If you have rather inadequate space but a number of friends whom you would like to invite to a meal, then the answer is an informal luncheon or evening buffet. In this way you can accommodate many more guests. It is, however, important to appreciate that people will want somewhere to sit, even if it is a buffet party, and they will need something on which to put glasses and plates of food. Whilst women seem to be able to balance plates quite happily on their laps, very few men are adept at this. You will find more detailed suggestions of the kind of food for buffets in the section beginning on page 55. In this, the recipes are based upon boned meats and poultry and the kinds of food that, although sustaining enough for a satisfying meal, are easily eaten with a fork.

Another form of entertaining for a number of people in a relatively small space is a drinks party. As this generally spans a fairly limited period, seating is less of a problem. The kind of food you serve must be easily eaten with the fingers as your guests will need to hold a glass and, in the case of women, probably a handbag as well. Recipes for this kind of party begin on page 56.

If you entertain quite a lot and want to avoid having exactly the same group of people on each occasion, a well-planned visitors' book will enable you to select guests who will enjoy each others' company.

Other information that may be included is what you wore at each party and any details of table settings etc. This will prevent every occasion being exactly like the last event.

When people come to stay make a note of any special needs; the kind of book they seem to enjoy reading; if they like early morning tea, breakfast in bed etc.

It is possible to buy books with spaces to fill in with this information, or quite easy to make up your own visitors' book.

Duration of the Party

When you invite guests to dinner, it is rather difficult to have any idea of how long it will continue; it is not usual, therefore, to give the duration of a dinner party. If, however, you plan a buffet or drinks party it is quite acceptable to indicate the time when this will begin and end. A drinks party generally covers a period of about two hours, so your invitation should say quite clearly: '12 noon - 2pm' or '6pm - 8pm'.

Every hostess has had experience of guests who linger. This may be a compliment to the pleasant atmosphere created by the host or hostess and may not matter in the slightest. It does happen occasionally that people just stay and stay and show no inclination to move.

This is extremely difficult for any host or hostess, for you cannot ask people to go, although it is singularly rude for guests to linger after the indicated time, unless asked to do so. There are various reasonably tactful ways of showing that the party is over:

1 stop offering any more drinks;

2 simply say: 'I am terribly sorry — I don't want to rush you, but we do have another appointment';

3 quite quietly, not showing any sign of annoyance, begin to pick up ashtrays, used glasses, etc and smilingly say to the lingering guests: 'You will forgive me if I just clear up a little'.

Those Special Touches

There are some houses one may visit where, although the surroundings, furnishings and food are beautiful, there is a lack of a welcoming atmosphere and it is very difficult for a guest to feel 'at home'. This may be due to the fact that the host and hostess are not particularly relaxed people, but it can be that too little thought has been given to the finer points of entertaining, ie those special and individual touches which do so much to assure visitors that they are truly welcome.

When you have people for a meal, or to stay, check upon any special dietary needs or particular dislikes; this does not mean discussing the entire menu you intend to serve, but just a brief remark in the letter or telephone call of invitation saying 'is there anything you cannot eat?'.

If your guests are staying overnight or for a longer period, take a long look at your guest room; imagine you are going to sleep there and consider these points:

Is the light by the bed sufficiently good for reading; and the light by the dressing table adequate for putting on make-up?

Are there enough covers on the bed? Your guests may be people who feel the cold and an extra blanket can easily be removed if the room is too warm.

Have you put some reading material beside the bed? If your guest's taste in reading is not known, have a selection of books and magazines.

Whilst your guests may not wish to eat or drink at night time or early in the morning, it is a good idea to have a small tin of biscuits or a plate of fruit in the guest room together with a jug of drinking water. If you have a spare electric kettle or a modern teamaker you could put this in the guest room, together with the equipment for making tea or coffee. This gives a lovely feeling of freedom to any guest.

Check upon whether your guests like breakfast in bed or would rather come downstairs; to some people a meal in bed is a real luxury, to others both unwelcome and tiresome.

Advise your guests of the availability of hot water for baths, and the bathroom. In a busy household where members of the family have to go to work or school it is extremely worrying if they cannot get into the bathroom at the right time. It is quite easy to ask a guest 'Do you like your bath at night or in the morning?' and, having ascertained their preference, indicate a good time to choose.

Even if you do not smoke, make quite sure there are adequate ashtrays available for your guests in case they wish to smoke.

Check on the comfort of chairs in the sitting room. Often one tends to use the same chair; try out the remaining seats in the room and move cushions around if you feel this is necessary.

(opposite) Moules à la Marinière (see page 74)

10

Issuing Invitations

This is an era of informality and many invitations are issued on the telephone; when you do this it is wise to repeat both the day *and* the date of the party, eg Tuesday, the sixteenth of December, to avoid needless confusion. Give a clear idea of the time the party begins and ends if it is a drinks party, together with any details, such as whether it is to be a dressed-up affair or quite an informal occasion.

If you issue a written invitation this can be written in the form of a chatty letter or a formal card. You can buy printed invitation cards of many designs and all you need to do is fill in the details. If, however, you write your own formal invitation it should look rather like this:

George and Mary Jones
invite
Bob and Ellen Smith
to a dinner party
on
Tuesday, 16th December
at 7.30 pm
Dress: Informal   RSVP

The RSVP does mean you request a reply, and the majority of people will do this quickly. If, however, the party time is coming very near and you have not heard from anyone, then it is advisable to telephone or write. The tactful approach is to query whether your invitation was delayed or lost in the post.

Making Introductions

Modern etiquette is less formal than in the past, but is still an important part of party-giving. The recognised form of introduction is to introduce a man to a woman, ie 'May I introduce (or present) Mr John Brown' then continue 'Mrs Mary Smith'. Although correct, this does little to facilitate conversation between the two guests. One important rule, particularly at an informal buffet or drinks party where you must circulate and leave each group of people to talk, is to give some idea of their interests so that a better introduction in this case would be: 'May I introduce John Brown, who is a superb gardener' then continue 'John, this is Mary Smith (or Mrs Mary Smith, if you want to be more formal) who will, I know, be interested in your garden, as she takes classes in flower arranging'. You hope this introduction will provide an immediate basis on which the two people can start a conversation.

Another accepted courtesy is to introduce a younger person to an older person of the same sex, for example: 'May I introduce Julia Jones, who was at school with my daughter, Alison. She is reading English at university'; then continue 'Julia, this is Mrs Mary Brown, who teaches flower arranging'. There may seem little relationship between an English degree and the floral arts but the older woman should be able to direct the conversation towards teaching, learning and university life. Mrs Brown also has been given another topic of conversation, ie to enquire about Alison.

If one of your guests has a title then other people are introduced to him or her: 'Sir John, may I present (or introduce) Bill Robinson, who is a colleague of my husband', then continue 'Sir John Brown has been the British Consul in Tangier for many years'.

Seating Arrangements

It is considered correct for the hostess to have the most important gentleman on her right and the next most important gentleman on her left. The host has the most important lady on his right and the next most important lady on his left. Obviously these seating arrangements may not always work out satisfactorily if you have an odd number of people at the table.

3 Practical Points

This chapter covers the various practical aspects of entertaining that need to be considered. Firstly, setting the table for various types of entertaining, then suggestions that enable you to make some preparations ahead of the occasion.

The latter part of the chapter deals with the prevention of accidents in your home and then gives speedy ways to deal with any mishap that may have occurred.

Laying the Table

A well-laid table is an intrinsic part of a delicious meal. Nowadays many homes use linen or other fabric for table mats and the diagram below shows how the table can be laid, when using mats. If your table is relatively small you may find that such a number of mats looks slightly crowded and a tablecloth gives a neater appearance. Two ways of arranging the cutlery for a formal meal are given; you will find that the second method gives a less cluttered look to the table. In addition to the cutlery for each individual place, sufficient serving spoons, or forks and spoons, should be arranged on the table, sideboard or on the Hostess heated food trolley. You need these for serving vegetables, sauces and desserts. Put the carving knife or knives and fork ready for cutting meat and poultry.

Always protect your polished table with heat-resistant mats; place these under the fabric mats or the tablecloth.

If you have attractive heat-resistant mats and a beautiful table, then use these and do not cover them with fabric mats or a tablecloth.

Place table napkins (serviettes) on the side plate, as illustrated on page 14. If you have stiff cotton or linen napkins they can be folded as the sketches below, so that they stand upright. First fold the napkin into a triangle, then bring points A and D together.

The Way to Serve Foods

Serve a mixed hors d'oeuvre with a small knife and fork, or a fish knife and fork. Blend the cold ingredients with mayonnaise or oil and vinegar, if using these; it is not usual to serve separate salad dressings with an hors d'oeuvre.

Halve avocados, remove the stones. Top the fruit with a dressing, lemon juice or topping, see pages 59 and 61. Serve with a teaspoon or teaspoon and small fork.

Halve fresh grapefruit, loosen the fruit segments with a grapefruit knife or any sharp knife and remove the pips. Put the halved fruit into sundae glasses or small dishes, chill in the refrigerator. Decorate with Maraschino or glacé cherries. Serve with a grapefruit spoon (like a teaspoon but with a sharper point) or a teaspoon. Put a sugar dredger filled with caster sugar on the table in case some people like sweetened grapefruit. Newer ways of serving grapefruit are on page 59.

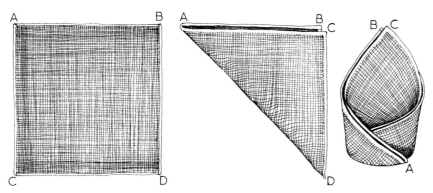

Softer material, or paper napkins can be folded into neat triangles.

The Way to Serve Foods

Cut large melons into thick slices, remove the seeds, then slice the pulp down to the skin. Decorate each portion with a ring of orange and a Maraschino or glacé cherry.

Serve with a small, or fruit, knife and fork or a dessert spoon and fork. Always chill melon for 1-2 hours.
Halve small melons, or cut a slice from individual-sized fruit. Remove the seeds. Serve with a dessert spoon and fork. The centre of the halved or whole melon can be filled with port wine.
Another way to serve melon is to dice the pulp or form this into balls with a vegetable scoop, put into glasses and moisten with a little sherry.
Put containers of sugar and ground ginger on the table to serve with the melon.
Asparagus and Jerusalem artichokes are generally eaten with the fingers, so that individual finger bowls should be placed before each guest. These are a relic of a bygone age, so may not be available. Use attractive soup bowls as a substitute. Fill with warm water and float a small flower on top. Pages 62 and 96 give ways to cook these delicious vegetables.

Place Setting

The sketch below shows the popular method of laying one place setting. There are three glasses; the tumbler for water, one glass for white wine and the other for red wine. The cutlery, except for the dessert spoon and fork, is arranged in the order in which the food is eaten.

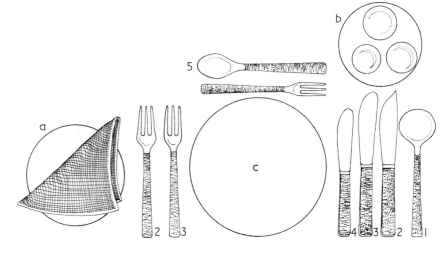

a Side plate and napkin **b** Small mat (coaster) and glasses
c Place mat
1 Soup spoon **2** Fish knife and fork **3** Knife and fork for main course
4 Cheese knife **5** Dessert spoon and fork

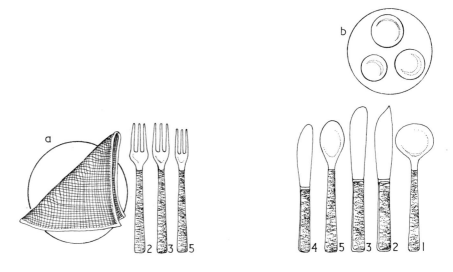

In this sketch the cutlery, side plate and glasses are arranged on a tablecloth. The dessert spoon and fork are placed inside the knife and fork for the main course. This looks a somewhat bewildering array of cutlery, but you always work from the outside inwards. The cheese knife is sometimes placed on the side plate.

14 (*opposite*) *Turkey Stroganoff, Turkey and Walnut Croquettes, Winter Salad and Crunchy Chicken Salad (see pages 86, 87, 95 and 99)*

The Way to Serve Foods

Cooked corn on the cob may be put on special holders, as the sketch below.

If you do not possess corn on the cob holders, then insert a metal skewer through the centre of the cooked cob. Serve with melted butter. Hold the skewer, or special holders with the fingers.

Unshelled, cooked Mediterranean prawns are often served with mayonnaise as an hors d'oeuvre.

While oysters can be cooked, they are such a luxury that they are generally served uncooked. Garnish the oysters with halved lemons, serve with cayenne pepper and brown bread and butter. The oysters will be opened by the fishmonger and should be served on the half shell.

If lobster is served cold, it is usual to keep this in its shell. Prepare the lobster as page 74, crack the claws in the kitchen with a light weight. Serve with lobster picks, or tiny forks, which can pull the flesh from the shell quite easily.

If you intend to serve escargots (snails), then you must invest in the proper holders and tiny forks to ease them out of their shells.

Corn on the cob, prawns, oysters, cold lobster and snails are handled with the fingers, so finger bowls must be provided.

A Buffet Setting

When you lay the table it is better to have the cutlery arranged as above. It is a good idea to divide each kind of food between two or three dishes to avoid congestion. If you push the table against a window or wall this gives more room in front of the table; place flowers at the back of the table. A beautifully ironed sheet makes an excellent covering for the table, if you do not possess a sufficiently large cloth.

Selecting Glasses

If you possess a range of glasses serve drinks in a traditional shape. If, on the other hand, you are buying new glassware and want to be economical, select tulip-shaped glasses on stems. All wines can be served in these. Information on serving wine is on page 29.

Sherry   Port wine or Madeira   Whisky   Tumbler for gin and tonic

Champagne   White wine   Red wine

Hock   Brandy   Liqueur   Tulip

16

Avoiding Accidents

Accidents often happen when you are rushed and trying to do too much too quickly, so give yourself as much time as possible for preparing, cooking and serving the meal.

When preparing vegetables do use good kitchen tools. Sharp knives are more efficient and you are less likely to cut yourself with them. When cooking, make certain that all pans are securely on the cooker with handles turned inwards.

Give yourself plenty of time to dish-up. This is the advantage of being able to keep food hot before your guests arrive. You will find information about this on pages 40 to 47. It is when one rushes out into the kitchen between courses that accidents can occur. If you have to do so, take another minute or so. Your guests would prefer a slight delay plus a calm, happy hostess to one who is worried and has, perhaps, dropped or spilt something. When dishing-up be sure you have good oven gloves available so that you hold hot tins, etc securely. If you are entertaining a lot of people you will find pots and pans surprisingly heavy, so make quite certain you grip these firmly before you strain the food in them.

Check on the temperature of serving dishes. Accidents happen when very hot food is put into an unwarmed serving dish. In the same way, you should chill dishes for iced desserts in the refrigerator to prevent these cracking.

Check that you have sufficient heat-resistant mats under the tablecloth or fabric mats, not only on the table but anywhere else you may be placing hot dishes. It is easier to avoid heat marks than to remove them. Make certain that surfaces in the sitting room are protected from damp glasses. Put out small glass mats before your guests arrive, for nothing is more disconcerting than a hostess who rushes round 'doling-out' mats when her guests are there; it rather implies that they are going to spill something. Provide plenty of ashtrays for smokers; keep a watchful eye for lighted cigarettes and cigars that might have been put down carelessly.

When placing bottles of wine, etc on the table, make certain that they are not near the edge; a sudden quick movement could knock them over. Invest in a good corkscrew. When opening bottles of wine do this slowly and carefully. When opening Champagne, or other sparkling wines, first get a table napkin. Have several glasses ready. Do not shake the bottle as you bring it from the ice bucket or refrigerator. Remove the outer foil from the cork, together with the wire cage surrounding the cork. Then, with the aid of the napkin, ease — but do not attempt to pull — the cork out of the bottle. Keep the neck of the bottle pointing away from your face or any person, but straight upwards. Should the cork be difficult to remove, a pair of nutcrackers, or the correct champagne opener (these look very like nutcrackers) will allow you gently to twist out the cork. As soon as the cork comes out, the bubbling champagne should be poured into the glasses so that none is wasted.

If An Accident Happens

Try to keep quite calm and not become upset; it *is* distressing to have a beautiful glass or piece of china broken, but nothing will bring this back, and you will only spoil the party atmosphere.

Remember, if you are trying to remove a stain from any material, work from the outside towards the centre of the stain so this is not spread.

If food is spilled on a dress or suit, wipe away the solid matter with soft paper, then sponge with a piece of cotton wool or a clean handkerchief dipped in cold water. Place another piece of white cotton (a second handkerchief) under the garment so that you do not spread the stain or make underclothes wet. Alcohol or other liquids are dealt with in the same way.

If the accident has happened to a guest it may be sensible to persuade them to borrow a dressing gown or housecoat, so that you can deal with the stain more efficiently. Washable articles should be put into a cold or warm detergent solution which is then brought up to the highest temperature recommended for the particular fabric. If the garment has to be dry-cleaned, advise the cleaners of the origin of the stain.

If alcohol has been spilt on a carpet, wipe this immediately with a clean, damp cloth. Red wines can be removed quite easily if you use a mild detergent solution. Dissolve washing-up liquid in hand-hot water, take just the lather from the top of the solution and rub away the stain; in this way you do not soak the carpet. There

17

are other recommended methods of dealing with red wine stains, eg sponge with white wine, put ice cubes over the stain, but the lather method is the easiest. Use a grease solvent for any grease marks.

If, in spite of precautions, you find a slight heat mark on a polished surface, treat it as soon as you can after your guests have departed. Rub the mark gently and firmly with linseed or olive oil on a soft cloth, then use furniture polish or a good furniture cream. You may have to do this several times, so do not get depressed if the mark does not come out at once. Bad heat marks need professional treatment.

A white ring made by liquid can generally be removed by the same method as recommended above. There are, however, excellent tinted liquids for furniture that help to cover marks.

If a Fire Occurs

A compact fire extinguisher is a valuable asset in any home and this should be used according to the directions.

If a pan of oil or fat catches fire NEVER try and move the pan or place it under water. Put a large lid or tin over the burning pan immediately. This should smother the flames.

Cutting and Carving

Many accidents occur when meat, poultry or game are cut or carved. The technique of cutting or carving requires a certain amount of knowledge about the bone construction of the joint or bird so that you cut or carve around, or between, the bones. A knife tends to slip if it hits the bone.

When cutting food in the kitchen select a really sharp-edged knife and place the meat or poultry on to a firm chopping board. When dividing poultry or game into portions, insert the tip of the knife between the joints *before* you commence cutting. This will enable you to ascertain exactly *where* you need to cut. As you begin cutting the poultry or game joints with the knife in your one hand, gently ease the joint away from the body with the second hand. Use firm movements with the knife and keep the blade pointing away from you. Raw or cooked poultry or game can be jointed with poultry scissors rather than a knife.

When carving in the kitchen or the dining room you must have good equipment. Use a really well-sharpened carving knife; use more than one knife when carving hot meat or poultry for a large number of people. The hot flesh blunts the cutting edge of a knife, so that it becomes less efficient; you should carve half the meat with the first knife, then change to the second knife. Keep all carving knives well-sharpened. If you use an electric carving knife follow the manufacturer's instructions.

It is essential to invest in a carving fork, and use one with a proper guard at all times. If the carving knife should slip it will strike the guard of the fork and no accident should occur.

Many modern stainless steel meat dishes have small spikes on the surface which hold the meat or poultry firmly in position; these spikes help to make carving easier and safer.

Danger From Heat

Fire is always a danger, but particularly so when a lot of people are moving around in a confined space. Make quite certain there are no unguarded open fires or portable heaters that can be knocked over.

If you use a table cooker or fondue heater in the dining room, keep this away from curtains, or the edge of the table where it may be knocked over. The continual heat from this type of cooker or a Hostess heated food cabinet could harm a highly polished or sensitive surface, such as a dining-room table, so protect this with heat-resistant mats.

Never under-estimate the danger from candles. They can be knocked over, or a sudden draught may blow the flame against curtains or the Christmas tree. If candles are left burning for some hours they can create an appreciable heat.

(opposite) Chicken Basquaise on a Hostess heat tray (see page 86)

Putting It Right

From time to time even the most accomplished and experienced cook has a failure in the kitchen. What appears at first glance to be a spoiled dish may well be disguised, or the fault remedied, with a little 'know-how'. I hope the following hints will be helpful.

The Fault	The Remedy
Hors d'oeuvre A fish cocktail sauce tastes dull.	*Hors d'oeuvre* Add a few drops of Tabasco, soy or Worcestershire sauce, plus a little cream.
A pâté has been over-cooked and is dry and crumbly.	Put the pâté into a bowl, stir in cream plus a little sherry or brandy until of the desired consistency. Add extra seasoning plus chopped herbs to taste.
Soups The soup is over-salt.	*Soups* Add a little milk or cream and taste again. If this has not remedied the fault, peel and dice one or two potatoes, simmer in the soup for 10-15 minutes, then lift out the potatoes, add more cream or milk. By this time the soup could have become too thin in consistency so a little extra thickening may be necessary.
The soup lacks flavour and time is short.	Add a little garlic and/or celery salt to a creamy soup; a pinch of curry powder and a little Worcestershire sauce to a meat-based soup; tomato purée is another excellent ingredient to add to meat or vegetable soups.
The soup looks dull.	Add an interesting garnish such as yoghurt and diced fresh or canned red pepper to a dark-coloured soup; browned blanched almonds are an ideal topping for creamy soups. Try tiny balls of cream cheese on a bortsch.
Sauces (These often cause problems) Sauce made with a roux (butter and flour) has formed lumps.	*Sauces* Whisk the sauce briskly and quite often the lumps will go. If this technique fails then rub the sauce through a sieve or put it into a liquidiser and switch on for a few seconds. This treatment will produce a smooth sauce, but one that becomes thinner in consistency, so allow it to simmer gently for a time so it will become a little thicker.
Sauce too thick.	Whisk in extra liquid, but taste the sauce after doing this to make certain there is adequate seasoning and flavouring.
Sauce too thin.	Either allow the sauce to cook for a longer period or allow 1 level teaspoon of cornflour to each 150ml (¼pt) of the sauce. You will need to blend the cornflour with 2-3 tablespoons of milk, cream or stock, depending upon the type of sauce. Whisk this into the hot, but not boiling, sauce and stir until thickened. A more subtle method of thickening the soup is to blend an egg yolk with a little milk, cream or stock, whisk this into the hot soup and simmer gently for a short time.
Hot sauce containing egg curdles.	Whisk very hard or treat as lumpy sauce above.
Mayonnaise sauce curdles during mixing.	Put an egg yolk into a basin and gradually whisk the curdled mayonnaise on to this.

The Remedy

Do not stir the sauce, pour into a clean saucepan, taste very critically and you may find the flavour unimpaired. If there is a very slight taste, a little extra flavouring and seasoning (or sugar, in the case of a sweet sauce) may disguise this. Put plenty of salt and cold water into the burned pan and leave it to soak.

Fish Dishes

Use extra melted butter in the sauce or topping to counteract the dry texture. Lift the fish on to heated individual plates, so there is no fear of the fish breaking again. Garnish attractively to disguise slight tendency of portions to break.

Meat or Poultry Dishes

Dish up the remainder of the meal into a Hostess trolley or cabinet and allow the joint or poultry to continue cooking. If time is short, carve the poultry or the joint, arrange on a flame-proof dish and cook under the grill for a short time.

Pastry Dishes

Take a grater and rub the fine side gently and carefully over the burned portion until removed. Dust sweet pastry with sieved icing sugar or brush the pastry on a savoury dish with a little beaten egg yolk and return to the oven for a short time to give a pleasant shine to the roughened pastry.

Gently cut the pastry into portions, then arrange on the fruit or savoury mixture as the sketch. This makes an interesting-looking dish and one that is easy to serve.

The Fault

Sauce burns in pan.

Fish Dishes

Fish slightly over-cooked and dry, also inclined to break.

Meat or Poultry Dishes

Rest of meal ready but joint or roast poultry under-cooked.

Pastry Dishes

Pastry slightly over-cooked and burned at the edges.

Pastry topping on a pie loses its shape.

4 Floral Arrangements

Choose this Japanese arrangement to create a striking result with few flowers.

A concealed pinholder helps to support stems at various angles.

Flowers, or an artistic blending of flowers and leaves, or fruit or candles, should provide a focal point in the various rooms, or on the dining table. Containers of flowers and plants play an important part in making your home look attractive. Your guests will undoubtedly regard it as a compliment that you have spent time and trouble in creating pleasing floral arrangements.

Perhaps the term 'floral arrangement' implies a complicated and elaborate display, worthy of a professional. This is not necessary; flowers are naturally beautiful and simple arrangements can be delightful.

It does, however, take a certain amount of time to prepare even the simplest vase of flowers, so it is advisable to pick, or buy, the flowers and leaves the day before the party. This will enable you to prepare the flowers, as in the information given in the next paragraph; work out the way in which you will fill the container and finally put the flowers in position. In most cases flowers benefit by being arranged 24 hours ahead; buds will open more fully and provide greater colour and beauty.

Preparing the Flowers

Whether you buy or pick flowers, there are certain points to remember. The blooms should be young, unless you are creating a very special effect, so they will last for as long a period as possible, but choose buds that are starting to open; tightly closed buds will not give the colourful effect you need. Never pick flowers or leaves in the heat of the day, but first thing in the morning. Prepare the flowers as soon as possible after purchasing or picking them. In order to prepare the flowers so they look beautifully fresh, check first on the flower stems; if these seem dry at the base cut away a small amount, then split the stems upwards for 1-2.5cm (½-1in) to enable the flowers to take up water. When stems are very hard and difficult to cut, they may need a light crushing. Place the flowers and leaves into a deep container of water and leave for 1-2 hours, or even longer in hot weather or when the flowers seem particularly limp. While cold water can be used, tepid water generally revives blooms better.

(opposite above) A simple but effective low arrangement suitable for a dining table of carnations with contrasting ferns and eucalyptus leaves

(opposite below) An elegant arrangement of gladioli, chrysanthemums, hydrangeas and dried grasses, contrasted with striking begonia leaves

22

Blend fruit with flowers for additional interest. Some fruits can be frosted.

Frosted Fruits

Grapes, red and blackcurrants, strawberries and other berry fruits look most attractive when coated with a light frosting. Beat an egg white lightly until it becomes slightly frothy. Brush this over the fruit with a small paint or pastry brush, then shake icing sugar through a very fine sieve so that it coats the fruit.

Use within 24 hours. After this time the coating can become rather sticky and the fruit deteriorates.

Selecting the Container

The choice of container will obviously depend upon the position in which the floral arrangement will stand and the kind of flowers available. It is important that the vase, or other container, should stand firmly when there are to be a number of people in the room to avoid any possibility of it being knocked over. The sketches, shown on this and page 22 show some unusual and practical containers that might be selected.

It is easier to anchor flowers and hold them in interesting and graceful positions if you use a pinholder or the modern blocks, such as Oasis. These are moistened and retain the water. If you do not possess either a pinholder or Oasis and want to support the flowers or leaves, there are occasions when you can substitute a well-scrubbed potato. It is not possible to insert delicate stems into the potato, but this is excellent for flowers or leaves with firm woody stems.

New Ideas For Floral Arrangements

Do not be too conservative in your designs.

If you have relatively few flowers follow the traditional Japanese method of arrangement illustrated in the left hand column where the few flowers and leaves give a striking outline.

Add fruit to the flowers: rosy apples blend well with red and gold flowers; bunches of white or black grapes hang gracefully among flowers and leaves. The grapes could be frosted, as described in the column on the left.

Use leaves and berries with, or instead of, the flowers. Most gardens can yield a variety of leaves of different shapes and colours. In autumn you will find seed heads and berries ideal for original, and economical, arrangements.

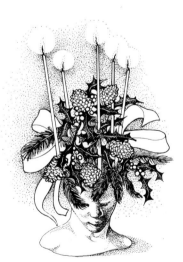

This arrangement of holly and candles would be ideal for Christmas.

Spray leaves with silver or gold aerosol, obtainable from most florists; it is particularly suitable for Christmas decorations.

5 Perfect Menus

When you plan a party menu there are a number of factors to consider in order to produce a first-class meal.

Firstly, you must think about the likes and dislikes of your guests and family. Naturally, you will avoid any foods or flavourings that are not popular, and you will desire to include one or more of their favourite foods, if these are in season and blend well with the rest of the menu. If in doubt as to your guests' tastes it is better to avoid the foods shown on the right, and continued on page 26.

Next consider your own cookery skills, as though you were assessing the ability of a stranger. What are the dishes you make best? Would it be a good idea to include these in the menu? If they seem a little plain, or ordinary, you can 'dress them up' with interesting garnishes, decorations or accompaniments. You may, for example, make exceptionally good pastry; if this is the case, incorporate pastry into one of the courses.

Jot down your thoughts on the ideal menu for the occasion; look at the dishes you have selected, check that all the foods required for these are readily available and can be purchased at a price you can afford. Having decided there are no problems about the food or the shopping for this menu, assess its value as a whole. These are the questions to ask youself.

Is it really interesting? A good menu must have an element of surprise; it should have slightly unexpected touches. If your menu appears to lack these it may well be possible to add a sauce, an accompaniment, a garnish or decoration, that achieves the originality you desire without changing the basic dishes.

Have you a good balance of flavours? No one course should have such a strong taste that every other dish seems dull and flavourless. It is also a mistake for every dish to be very rich, with a high proportion of cream or butter; if it is, then the meal becomes too cloying. All you would need to do in this case is to change one course, so that you introduce a fresh fruit flavour, or a dish with a refreshing bite.

Does the menu have changes of texture as well as flavour? Is every course soft and delicate? If the answer is 'yes' then either change one course, add crisp garnishes or decorations, or have a really crunchy salad with the hors d'oeuvre or main course. On the other hand, you do not want each course to consist of crisp, hard foods. If all dishes seem to have a firm texture, ring the changes with soft, creamy vegetables or sauces.

Conjure up the appearance of each dish in the menu; imagine how these will look on the table. Have you chosen to make up recipes that give a variety of pleasing colours? If you feel the food will taste good, but look dull, it is probably not necessary to make major changes but

Less Popular Foods

Avocados are a fruit that people either enjoy very much or dislike intensely. If you intend to serve these and do not know if all your guests like them, have other fruit, such as grapefruit or melon, available.

Eggs are such a usual food that it is difficult to visualise that some guests may dislike them intensely, or be allergic to them. Have a second hors d'oeuvre available if you plan an egg dish to start the meal.

Avoid escargots (snails) unless you are sure all your guests are happy about eating them.

Curries are generally popular in spite of their strong taste, but it is wise to check that everyone will enjoy this dish.

Fish is a fairly 'safe' food, and enjoyed by most people. Some people are allergic to shellfish, so have an alternative available.

Less Popular Foods

Meat or poultry are rarely unpopular, and would be most people's choice for the main dish. Vegetarians should let you know their prohibitions when accepting your invitation. You will find special dishes for vegetarians on page 98. Game, on the other hand, is sometimes a less popular food. If you do select game birds, venison or hare, do not allow them to hang for too long a period and so acquire an ultra-strong taste, unless you are confident that all your guests will appreciate this. Some vegetables and herbs may cause certain problems; for example aubergines (egg plants), courgettes and spinach are among the least popular. The solution is simple; have a reasonable selection of vegetables. Be sparing in your use of garlic, tarragon and fennel, the most definitely flavoured herbs.

Many people today are not over-fond of rich, creamy desserts, either because they are trying to lose weight or because they genuinely dislike sweet things. Offer the cheese board or fresh fruit at the same time as the dessert.

You may find your guests refuse alcohol before, or with, the meal. This may be because they are driving home; do not exert pressure upon them to change their minds. Offer well-chilled fruit juice or mineral water. Perrier is one brand of sparkling mineral water and Vichy or Malvern two readily available still mineral waters.

Coffee is, to most people, a perfect ending to a good meal. However, it may not agree with some of your guests, particularly when it is served late in the evening. Be prepared, therefore, to offer tea as an alternative.

simply to consider each individual dish and decide how it can be made more colourful. Do not, however, make the all-too-common mistake of over-garnishing and over-decorating food.

Last, but certainly not least, ask yourself if the meal will be satisfying. If it seems over-light and lacking in substance you may need to add an extra course, or additional vegetables. Do not, on the other hand, produce a menu where each dish is so substantial that no-one can eat the whole meal without feeling grossly over-fed.

There are a number of menus in Chapter 5.

Having decided on the final menu, check your store cupboard, freezer and refrigerator, then list the shopping you have to do. Reminders about shopping for perishable foods are given with the menus on pages 48 to 55. As the time of the party draws nearer, list the working order, also covered for the menus in this book on pages 48 to 55, and consider any problems about dishing-up and keeping the food looking perfect until it is to be eaten. This is one of the problems for a busy cook-cum-hostess and is fully discussed in this chapter (see pages 42 to 47).

The points given above, and on page 25, could be called the 'backbone' of a successful party. These are the essential points to consider at the beginning.

You are now ready to think about the drinks that you will serve; the choice of alcohol is covered very fully on the pages that follow. Buy, or order, wines well ahead so that you can prepare these properly. The interesting extras can be purchased, such as chocolates or petits fours to serve with the coffee.

I have stressed that you should think about the appearance of each dish and whether it will look colourful or dull. You can enhance the colour of the food by the mats or tablecloth and the flowers you choose for the room and table. You may like to keep to a colour scheme; for example, have everything pale green and yellow, a delicate combination on a hot day. In the middle of winter, when everything is rather dull outside, it is cheering to have bright colours in the food, china and table decorations. If you plan these ideas early it will give you time to shop around for the right kind of flowers, or to look round your own garden to see what is available.

Preparing Wines

Most sherries are at their best when served at cellar temperature, ie about 10.0-10.5°C (50-51°F) although there is a modern and pleasant vogue to lightly chill Tio Pepe, Fino's and other dry sherries.

White wines, including Champagne, must be well chilled but never over-chilled or iced. This destroys the flavour. If the wines have been stored in a cold place, where the temperature is about 6-7°C (43-45°F), then extra chilling should be unnecessary. If you need to chill the wine, allow approximately one hour in the cabinet part of the refrigerator (keep the bottle away from the freezing compartment), or a slightly shorter time in a deep ice bucket. This timing is suitable for most white wines, but German hocks can be chilled for a slightly shorter time and a sweet white wine, such as a Sauternes or Barsac, a

little longer. While you can decant a white wine, this is generally considered unnecessary.

Rosé wines are chilled in the same way as white wines. They must not be over-chilled, otherwise their singularly delicate flavour is lost.

Red wines should be served at room temperature. This is a fairly vague term and room temperatures vary considerably; the ideal, from the point of view of wine, is about 16.5-18.5°C (60-65°F), the slightly higher temperature being ideal for the heavier red wines. The exceptions to this are a very young Beaujolais, which can be chilled lightly, or a sparkling red wine, which is chilled as Champagne.

To make quite certain the wine is at an ideal temperature, bring it from a cool cellar or storage place the day before the party. Stand upright to allow any deposit to settle.

Red wines can be decanted, see comments on page 28. Draw the cork of a red wine several hours before the meal unless advised otherwise.

Apricot Brandy Coronet (see page 105)

27

Looking After Glassware

Beautiful wineglasses and decanters are worth cherishing, so wash and dry them carefully.

The rims of glasses easily become chipped, when put down on to a hard surface, so place a teacloth over the draining-board as the glasses drain.

It is important that wineglasses and decanters are washed in hot water only, rather than a detergent solution. If the smallest amount of detergent is left in a glass it can spoil the clarity and flavour of a wine and might well restrict the effervescence of sparkling wines.

To remove stains from the inside of a decanter, use a little bleach (the type of powder used to clean dentures is excellent) with hot water, then rinse well.

Buying the Drink

The drinks served at a party are nearly as important as the food, so give time and thought to their selection, especially if it falls to you to choose the wine, and you lack experience. It is wise to go to a good wine merchant where you can discuss the matter with the trained staff. They will want to know the food being served before making recommendations. Food and wine need to complement each other, although the rigid rules you may sometimes read, about the particular wine you *must* serve with a certain food, are not to be taken too seriously. There are good reasons for choosing a *type* of wine for each course, and these are explained on page 29, but if you have favourite wines that blend with your planned menu, serve these by all means.

Wine merchants offer an almost bewildering array of wines from many countries. The wines listed on the next page and page 31 are fairly well known, but they are both reliable and popular, and also readily available.

First consider the quantity of alcohol you will need. Obviously, this depends upon the occasion, but the following information gives some idea of the capacity of various bottles:

Sherry, port, Madeira: approximately 12 glasses per bottle.

White, rosé or red wines: approximately 6-8 glasses per bottle, and you need to allow about ½ bottle (3-4 glasses) wine per person at a dinner party. If serving white wine with the first course only, you may need just one glass per person and then more generous quantities of a red wine with the main course.

Champagne and sparkling wines: approximately 8 glasses per bottle.

Vermouth: 12 glasses if drunk by itself, but 24-30 if served with gin.

Spirits, such as gin, whisky, rum and vodka: 20-24 servings, but this varies a great deal.

Liqueurs: approximately 30 glasses per bottle.

In addition to the above you should stock up on soda water, tonic, bitter lemon, ginger ale and soft fruit drinks, tomato juice and fruit squash, if you are having a drinks party or a buffet meal. These may be less important when planning a dinner party at which wine only is served. You will need fresh lemons if you are offering gin, and fresh oranges if any of your guests are likely to choose Campari.

Decanting Wines

One reason for decanting is to make certain that any deposit in the wine is left in the bottle and the wine in the decanter is bright and clear. Some wines, port in particular, have a heavy deposit and decanting is an advantage. Before decanting a wine, allow the bottle to stand upright for several hours, so that any deposit sinks to the bottom. Make sure the decanter is clean, dry and well polished. Pour the wine into the decanter steadily and slowly. Do not shake the bottle as you do this, for this would disturb the sediment.

The second reason for decanting wine is to aerate it and most experts agree that this is the greater value of using a decanter for wine.

Selecting the Wine

The choice of wine is very much a personal taste; experts can offer advice, but everyone has their particular likes and dislikes and these should govern the final purchase.

Most people would, however, accept the fact that Champagne is the wine to select for a special occasion. It has no rival. The price today is very high, but you may find supermarkets offering popular Champagnes such as Moet, Laurent Perrier, Pol Roger (non-vintage) and Charles Heidsieck at competitive prices.

Most Champagne brought into Britain is dry, but check the label; it will clearly indicate whether the wine is dry, extra dry, extra sec (also dry). Demi- or très sec indicates a less dry wine. Some of the famous names in Champagne are Bollinger, Perrier-Jouet, Mumm, Heid-sieck-Dry-Monopole, Krug and Taittinger. Non-vintage Champagnes have a good flavour, if not as full as the rarer vintage wines.

If you do not want to buy Champagne but desire the excitement of a sparkling wine, look for the excellent French sparkling Vouvray, or Veuve du Vernay, or the popular Kriter. You will find the Italian sparkling Asti Spumante (rather sweet for many tastes) readily available, or look for the less well-known Cinzano Principe di Piedmonte. You also have a wide range of German sparkling hocks and Mosel (often spelt Moselle) wines from which to choose.

Wine merchants will show you sparkling white wines from various countries, so be prepared to try new names. For example, the Penedés area (in Catalonian Spain) produces excellent wines by the Champagne method, Freixenet being one of the best.

When buying wine allow yourself time to look around, to note, and discuss names that may be new to you. The lists below are fairly conservative because these particular wines are well distributed, but there are splendid wines from America (Californian wines are excellent), Australia and other countries available today.

Classified château-bottled wines are generally slightly better, more consistent in quality, but much higher in price, than the non-château-bottled wines. Be prepared to look for the cheaper alternatives.

About White Wines

From France, white Burgundies (dry wines) such as the superb Chablis, Meursault, Puligny-Montrachet, white Mâcons, Pouilly Fuissé and Pouilly Fumé (a white wine with a smoky taste), the Alsatian Rieslings (often drier than the German Riesling), Sylvaner and Traminer. White Bordeaux wines such as Graves, and the sweet Sauternes and Barsac. Remember that the Loire Valley white wines are good and comparatively reasonable. Muscadet is considered the finest of these.

From Germany, the wide variety of hocks and Mosel (Moselle) wines.

From Italy, the delicious Tuscany wines or the delicate-tasting Soave from Veneto.

From Spain, the excellent Torres Viña Sol or some of the white wine from the Rioja area.

Serving Wines

Invest in a good traditional corkscrew and practise opening wine so that you can draw the cork from the bottle easily and skilfully. If you are nervous about doing this in front of guests, it is reassuring to have red wine bottles ready opened, and you could draw the cork of white or rosé wines, then press it back into the top of the bottle. Broken corks cause many problems. Advice on opening Champagne is given on page 17. When the cork has been removed, wipe the neck of the bottle with a clean, dry table napkin. If, by some unhappy chance, the cork breaks when it is being drawn, remove the corkscrew and tiny pieces of cork that may be adhering to it, then try again. If the cork breaks and crumbles as it is withdrawn there will be a chance that pieces of cork may have fallen into the wine. In this case, simply strain the wine into a decanter. You may feel happier to take the bottle into the kitchen to do this. If you do not possess a decanter, strain the wine into a clean jug — after all, this is how wine is often served in France.

It is advisable for the host or hostess to pour a little wine into their own glass first, and taste it. (If the wine is decanted earlier, sip a little wine then.) This is not ill-mannered, simply a wise precaution to ensure that the wine tastes pleasant. When satisfied on this point, serve the wine to the guests. Keep a table napkin round the bottle as you pour; this saves any drips going on to the table mats or cloth. Return Champagne, or other wines that need to be kept cold, to the ice bucket.

About Rosé Wines

Rosé wines would be a good choice, particularly for summertime meals. The most popular rosé wines are the Portuguese Mateus, the French Tavel and Pradel, the Spanish De Casa Rosado and the rosé wines from the Bader district of Germany.

About Red Wines

The choice of a red wine will be important if this is to accompany the main course.

From France, the red Burgundies from such famous places as Beaune, Pommard, Nuits St George, Gevrey-Chambertin, Volney, Mâcon and the young Beaujolais, which are served at a cooler temperature than most red wines (see page 27). Sparkling Burgundies are less familiar, but would appeal to many people, and be a pleasing change. The clarets, ie the Bordeaux red wines, are very numerous; most wine merchants stock a range of the classed growth clarets from St Emilion, St Julien, St Estèphe, Pouillac and Medoc districts. Wine from the Margaux area is less readily available; do not confuse this with Château Margaux which, like other château-bottled clarets such as Lafite and Latour, can cost up to £30 a bottle. With the rising cost of wines from the traditional areas of France in recent years, more people in Britain are discovering the excellence of the red wines from the Rhône area; two quality names are Hermitage and Châteauneuf du Pape.

The Ahr and Adelmann areas of Germany provide good light red wines, and Italian Chianti is a general favourite. Do not disregard the robust 'Bull's Blood of Eger' red wines from Hungary.

Selecting Liqueurs

It is easy to acquire a large selection of liqueurs and yet find people select only one or two. This means you are left with full bottles of the less popular. Most liqueurs are rather sweet and some people dislike them. While there are tiny liqueur glasses in which to serve these drinks, you can pour a small quantity into a tulip-shaped glass. Brandy, port and Madeira are served in the glasses illustrated on page 16.

Brandies are made in most wine-growing countries but the finest, and therefore the most suitable as a liqueur, are Cognac and Armagnac. Pour a little brandy into a balloon glass. The drinker should cup the glass in his or her hand, so creating a little warmth, swirl the brandy around in the glass to release the bouquet, then drink it. Favourite fruit-flavoured brandies are apricot, cherry, peach and Grand-Marnier (orange-flavoured).

Curaçao (orange-flavoured liqueur) is also popular and sloe-gin makes an interesting liqueur. Whisky-lovers would probably select Drambuie. Other favourite liqueurs are Crème de Menthe (often served 'frappé', ie over crushed ice); Advocaat (a creamy egg drink); coffee-flavoured Kahlua or Tia Maria and Crème de Cacao (chocolate-flavoured).

If serving Madeira select the sweet Bual or Malmsey. Vintage port, a heavier wine than tawny port, has been a traditional drink at the end of a meal in Britain since the seventeenth century.

Making Canapés

The term 'canapés' is used to describe the small pieces of food served with drinks.

These can vary in many ways — the following are basic ideas which you can adapt according to personal taste and the ingredients available.

Miniature Kebabs

Put various ingredients on to cocktail sticks and press into a large cabbage, loaf of bread or grapefruit. Some of the most interesting combinations of colour and flavour are:
1 Miniature rolls of smoked salmon.
2 Balls of melon (made with a vegetable scoop) or diced melon and diced cooked ham or rolls of Parma ham.
3 Peeled prawns and cubes of pineapple.
4 Gherkins and peeled prawns.
5 Cream cheese, bound with a very little Mayonnaise, mixed with chopped nuts and rolled into balls with small gherkins and stuffed olives. Diced cheese could be used instead.

The base for canapés can be fried bread (this keeps crisp better than toast), toast, bread and butter (rye bread is particularly good), small crisp biscuits.
Top with:
1 Liver pâté, garnished with tiny pieces of gherkin, tomato or red pepper.
2 Smoked salmon, garnished with asparagus tips.
3 Soft cream cheese, topped with well-drained mandarin orange segments.
4 Sliced Danish Blue cheese garnished with de-seeded grapes.
5 Scrambled egg topped with anchovy fillets.

31

(opposite) Pineapple Nougat (see page 103)

Serving Aperitifs

If your guests will be eating lunch or dinner soon after their arrival there is no need to offer food with the aperitif; just supply dishes of olives, gherkins and nuts.

Madeira and Port Wine

The drier Madeira wines, or white port, are excellent chilled as sherry (see page 26).
Dry white vermouth, such as Martini or Noilly Prat, can be served neat in a small glass. Add a tiny piece of lemon 'zest', the top yellow part of the rind; twist this as you drop it into the glass, to extract a little oil of lemon. Decorate the glass with an olive on a cocktail stick. Gin with a little dry vermouth is popular. Sweeter red vermouths, when served neat, generally have a cocktail (Maraschino) cherry on a stick. Dubonnet and Campari are served with chilled soda or tonic water to provide a long drink. Put a slice of orange into Campari. Dubonnet is popular with bitter lemon. Most people enjoy ice in these drinks.
A less-known long drink is made by blending a little Campari into a tumbler of fresh orange juice.

To Serve Gin

Make sure that tonic water, soda water or bitter lemon is well chilled to serve with gin, and have slices of fresh lemon and ice available.
Another favourite way of serving gin is with lemon, orange or lime cordial.

To Serve Whisky

Some people enjoy whisky undiluted, but most prefer it with soda or just water. Ginger ale is another favourite accompaniment. Ice is often appreciated in whisky. Whisky and ice is called 'on the rocks'.

Selecting Aperitifs

You may have a very well-stocked cellar or drinks cupboard with a large range of alcohol, and be very experienced in offering a variety of drinks. This page is of more interest to people who have less experience in the selection of alcohol and the preparation of drinks.

An Aperitif

When you invite guests to a luncheon or dinner party it is usual to offer a drink as an aperitif (the definition of this term being a drink as an appetiser).

The perfect aperitif before a meal at which wine is to be drunk is Champagne, but in view of its prohibitive price today most people would select an alternative (Champagne, and other sparkling wines, are dealt with on page 29). Sherry, a fortified wine, would be the best alternative to offer. Purists would say it should be a dry sherry before a meal, and some of the indications of a dry sherry are given below.

Fino is dry, or very dry. One of the driest and best-known sherries is Tio Pepe; another is La Ina. Not everyone enjoys a very dry sherry. Amontillado is rarely as dry as a true Fino and is a wise choice if you plan to have just one sherry. One could call it a medium sherry; the wine merchant will recommend many sherries that fit into this category. Oloroso is a darker sherry, generally sweetened; many women prefer this type as an aperitif.

If you are offering sherry only, then you could have three types — very dry or dry, medium, and sweet; simply fill the sherry glasses or partially fill tulip glasses.

Vermouth and Bitters, such as Campari, have become very popular. These are basically wine to which herbs and spices have been added, giving an aromatic flavour. Vermouth used to be divided into two groups, 'French' — a dry white vermouth, and 'Italian' — a sweeter red vermouth (Rosso). The range is now fairly large and suggestions for serving these are given on the left. The best known names are Campari (strongly aromatic and non-sweet), Dubonnet (red and sweeter), Cinzano (dry white, or sweeter red), Riccadonna (obtainable as an extra dry or dry white or a sweeter red). The older favourites are Martini (dry white) and Noilly Prat (extra dry white).

Gin is enjoyed by many people as an aperitif. Methods of servings are given on the left.

Madeira wines are usually served at the end of a meal, but the driest, Sercial, or slightly less dry, Verdelho, are good alternatives to sherry as a prelude to the meal. They can also be served with certain soups, see page 33. White port is another unusual aperitif but it is excellent if served well chilled.

More Aperitifs

Some people will enjoy whisky, rum or vodka (see page 33). The least complicated aperitif is probably to have a bottle of the wine you intend to serve at the meal.

Do not disregard the fact that many people might prefer to drink lager, beer or cider before, and during, the meal, especially in hot weather. Serve these drinks chilled from the refrigerator. Remember that guests from America and Australia are used to having their beer very cold indeed. There is an enormous range of ciders available today, ranging from inexpensive flagons of dry and sweeter cider, to bottles of excellent vintage and Champagne cider.

Wine and Food
The reason why experts advise serving a white wine with fish and delicately flavoured meats, and a red wine with red meats, such as beef, is a wise one. Wine and food must be amicable partners at a meal; neither should dominate. If you serve a strongly-flavoured red wine with a fish dish you will be unable to appreciate fully the flavour of the food. In the same way, game and beef have such definite flavours that the wine to accompany these must be equally robust.

In each menu in the book you will find suggestions for the wines that would be a good choice. In most cases one or two wines only are given, since family entertaining seldom includes a different wine with each course. There may, however, be occasions when you are having a special celebration that warrants a gourmet's touch and the following gives the choice of wines to serve with each course.

Hors d'oeuvre
The wine served will depend upon the nature of the food. A sweet to medium sherry or Madeira blends with grapefruit or melon, although port wine is excellent with melon, especially if you have poured some over the fruit (see page 14).

Vegetables such as asparagus, or liver pâtés, blend with a dry white or rosé wine; the same wines can accompany a mixed hors d'oeuvre, or try a young Beaujolais when this is available.

Fish, particularly when smoked, eg smoked salmon and mackerel, is best with a dry sherry, hock or classic Chablis. Vodka makes a pleasing drink with caviare.

Soup
The wine served can vary with the ingredients used in the soup, but a dry sherry is a good choice, and so is a dry Madeira.

Fish
Select dry, or medium dry white wines, such as a white Burgundy or Loire wine (see page 29); the menus will suggest the actual wine names, as the ultimate choice will depend upon the kind of fish and flavourings in the sauce.

Meat
The choice of wine depends not only on the kind of meat, but also the way in which it is cooked.

Beef dishes really demand a red wine and this gives you an enormous range from which to choose. The stronger the flavour, ie beef casseroles, oxtail and goulash, the more robust the wine. All the red wines listed on page 31 would be suitable.

Lamb seems at its best with a good Bordeaux wine.

The choice of wine with pork varies according to the mode of cooking. Where you have apple or other fruit flavours with the meat

To Serve Rum
Rum is a less popular spirit for a straightforward drink, but a modern taste is for rum and Coke (Coca Cola).

To Serve Vodka
Opinions vary as to the virtues of vodka. Some experts dismiss this as a spirit without character. Others consider this a good aperitif — it has a clean taste and leaves no smell on the breath, so is ideal at lunch time. If serving vodka neat, it should be well chilled, and is usually drunk at one gulp. Your guests may like it as a longer drink with the same accompaniments as gin, or blended with tomato juice (called a Bloody Mary) or with ginger ale (called a Moscow Mule).

For Non-drinkers
Blend iced tonic water with a few drops of Angostura bitters.

To Serve Tomato Juice
Tomato juice is a favourite aperitif. Much of the bottled tomato juice is ready-seasoned. If you buy unflavoured canned or bottled juice you will need to make your own additions. A pinch of salt, celery salt and a shake of pepper produces very much more character in this juice. Most people like a little Worcestershire sauce. Add this drop by drop, stir well. Your guests may themselves prefer to add the amount of sauce they like.
Another very excellent flavouring for tomato juice is dry sherry. Use approximately half a sherry glass of the wine to a small glass of tomato juice.

The very effective Hostess Bar Trolley incorporates a large capacity ice container and ample room for storage and preparing drinks — enabling the host to stay at the heart of the party

you could serve a really dry white or rosé wine, although most people tend to select a red. If pork is served without stuffing or sauce, then certainly have a red wine.

Veal can be classed as poultry.

Poultry and Game
Chicken and turkey blend with most wines so you could continue to serve the white wine selected for fish, or change to any good red wine. The sauce often determines the choice of wine. Duck and goose are best with a dry white wine; those from the Alsace area would be excellent. Game really demands a fine red wine. Most people would choose a claret (Bordeaux wine).

National dishes, such as Spanish Paella, are best served with a wine of the country; these are suggested in the menus.

Desserts
This is the opportunity to enjoy the sweet white wines such as Sauternes, Barsac and Asti Spumante or to end the meal on a luxurious note with Champagne. The Hungarian Tokay is excellent with strongly-flavoured desserts.

34

(opposite) Mulled Cider Cup (see page 37)

Serving Wine Cups
The recipes on this page and continued on page 37, produce attractive-looking drinks. It is, therefore, worthwhile selecting the most attractive container for serving these. A large clear glass bowl is ideal or a silver punch bowl. The cold drink is served in wine or tulip glasses. If you do not possess a punch ladle then use a soup ladle instead.

Crushing Ice

It is very important that ice is not crushed in a liquidiser goblet as this blunts the blades. The best way to crush ice is to put the ice cubes on a folded clean teacloth, cover these with a second folded cloth, then tap them sharply with a light weight or wooden rolling pin. Gather up the broken ice and store in an insulated container until ready to use.
It is a good idea to prepare a quantity of ice cubes before a party. Put into a polythene container and spray with soda water to help keep them separated. Store in the freezer.

Filling Wineglasses

Most people like to be generous when serving food and drink, but do not make the mistake of filling wineglasses to the brim. Obviously this would make it almost impossible to lift the glass without spilling the wine. The other reason for not over-filling glasses is to leave space in the glass for the wine to breathe. It is considered ideal for the glasses to be no more than two-thirds full.

Cheese
Most strong cheeses 'kill' the flavour of most wines, except for a really good port, Madeira or Burgundy, that is why it is important to select the cheeses and wines carefully for a Cheese and Wine Party. Delicate cream cheeses blend well with younger red wines such as Beaujolais or with a white wine.

Coffee
This is the time to serve liqueurs, and various types are listed.

Cold Drinks

The following recipes, based mostly on wines, produce an interesting variety of drinks. Relatively small quantities are given, but it is easy to increase these for larger numbers. Multiply all ingredients to give a good balance of flavour.

Champagne Cocktail
Take a lump of sugar; rub over an orange or lemon until lightly coloured. Put into a Champagne glass, sprinkle the sugar with Angostura bitters. Add a little crushed ice and fill the glass with Champagne. Brandy is sometimes used instead of Angostura.

Buck's Fizz
Pour fresh orange juice into Champagne glasses, top-up with Champagne. The classic recipe uses one-third orange juice and two-thirds Champagne, plus a dash of Grenadine, but the proportions can vary according to personal taste.

Champagne Cup
Pare the rinds from an orange and a lemon. Squeeze out the juice from the fruits. Put the rinds with 25-40g (1-1½oz) sugar and 6tbspn water into a saucepan. Heat until the sugar has dissolved. Cool and strain over crushed ice in an attractive bowl. Pour in 1-2 wineglasses of brandy and the fruit juice, together with a sliced orange. Add a bottle of Champagne, then fill approximately 8 glasses. A sparkling white wine (see page 29) could be used instead of Champagne.

Kir
This name is given to a pleasant drink made by blending approximately 1tbspn of Cassis (the blackcurrant liqueur) with each glass of white wine. You may also find the name 'Kir' used to describe a blending of a red Bitters with white wine.

Claret Cup
Pare the rind from 2 lemons and 2 oranges, put these with 75g (3oz) sugar and 150ml (¼pt) water into a saucepan. Heat until the sugar has melted, cool and strain over crushed ice in a bowl. Add the lemon and orange juice and 2 bottles of claret (red Bordeaux). Float slices of cucumber, apple and sprigs of borage or mint on top. Just before serving, add approximately 600ml (1pt) soda water. This would fill about 20 glasses.

White Wine Cup
Follow the proportions in the Claret Cup, opposite, but omit the soda water. Use a little less sugar with a sweet wine. To give more flavour you could add 1 or 2 wineglasses of brandy, Curaçao or apricot brandy. Float strawberries or other summer fruits in this if in season.

More Cold Drinks

Rosé Wine Cup
All rosé wines are admirable for cold drinks. Use the Claret Cup recipe on the previous page but omit the soda water. To give more flavour add 1-2 wineglasses of cherry brandy. Float fresh cherries on top if in season.

Cider Cup
Cider makes a pleasant and economical cold cup. There are various kinds of cider, some sparkling, others more like a still wine; some ciders are very sweet, others dry. This means you need to adjust the recipe you use and suggestions for doing this are incorporated below. Do not make the mistake of imagining cider is an ideal drink for young people as some cider has a high alcoholic content. Bulmers make a sweet, sparkling apple drink, called Cidona, and this could be used to produce a non-alcoholic drink.

Pare the rinds from 2 lemons and 2 oranges. Put these into a saucepan with 150ml (¼pt) water or well-strained weak China tea and 25-50g (1-2oz) sugar; if using a dry cider increase the amount to 75g (3oz). Heat until the sugar has melted, cool and strain over crushed ice in a bowl. Add the lemon and orange juice and 2L (3½pt) cider. You can use slightly less cider and some apple juice to make up the quantity. Float slices of apple and sprigs of mint on top. If using a still cider you could add a small amount of soda water to the Cider Cup just before serving the drink. This produces about 16 glasses.

Hot Drinks

The recipes on the right of this page give the traditional mulled ale and wine, but cider, as in the recipe below, also makes an excellent hot drink. If serving hot drinks in glassware make sure this is heat-resistant, and warm it before adding the very hot liquid. You can, of course, use a silver punch bowl. The ingredients for the drink can be prepared, then brought just *to* boiling point immediately before serving.

Mulled Cider Cup
Cut 5 medium oranges into thin slices, quarter the slices from 3 of the oranges. Put approximately 3L (5¼pt) cider into a saucepan. Add 50-75g (2-3oz) brown sugar, the whole orange slices, 3-4 cloves, ¼tspn grated nutmeg and ¼tspn ground cinnamon. Bring the drink to the boil. Slice 1-2 dessert apples and 2 bananas, add to the hot drink just before serving. Keep the quartered orange segments to decorate the glasses. This makes 20-24 glasses. See colour picture on page 35.

Traditional Mulls

This word appears to have originated from the seventeenth century and describes a hot drink. In the old days a red-hot poker was put into the wine or other alcohol. Today, when pokers are almost extinct, it is advisable to bring the liquid to boiling point, but do not allow it to continue heating (see comments on left).

Mulled Ale
Heat together approximately 3L (5¼pt) strong dark ale with up to 300ml (½pt) brandy or rum, 6-8 cloves, a good pinch of ground ginger and ¼tspn ground cinnamon. Taste the drink as it heats and add about 50g (2oz) brown sugar. Serve in heated tankards. This gives 10-12 servings.

Mulled Red Wine
It was traditional to select a claret for this drink, but any full-bodied red wine or port or Madeira could be used. Pour 150ml (¼pt) water into a good-sized saucepan. Add 50g (2oz) white sugar or honey, the thinly pared rind of ½ lemon and ½ orange and a piece of cinnamon stick or a little ground cinnamon. Heat until the sugar has dissolved, then add a wineglass of brandy and a bottle of red wine. Bring to boiling point. Transfer to a warmed punch bowl and serve in warmed glasses. This gives 8-10 servings.

Helpful Hints

Special Guests

You may entertain people who have certain dietary problems, or beliefs. These will mean extra planning on the part of the hostess to ensure her guests enjoy the meal.

Vegetarians

Serve delicious salads; add nuts to make them satisfying. Concentrate on a generous selection of vegetables and fruit. Health food stores stock a wide range of vegetarian products.

Vegetarians

Most vegetarians are happy to eat dishes containing eggs and cheese and there are many delicious dishes based on these foods; a selection is given on page 98. Some vegetarians are just non-meat eaters and enjoy fish dishes. If you are told your guests are Vegans, this means they are very strict vegetarians and do not eat any animal product, including eggs, cheese or milk.

Jewish Guests

Shop for meat at a Kosher butcher, choose casserole-type meat dishes as the method of killing often results in drier meat that does not give the same succulent effect in roasting. Use oil or chicken fat in place of butter. Choose parve (a synthetic cream) instead of real cream. Most good delicatessen shops sell Jewish foods.

Jewish Guests

There are certain prohibited foods; these include shellfish, pork (ham and bacon) and any birds of prey. Meat and poultry (a general favourite) must be obtained from a Kosher butcher, and while beef, lamb and veal are allowed, the Jewish law only permits cuts from the forequarters of the animal.

One dietary ruling you must consider is that meat and dairy products cannot be used together in the same meal, so you cannot cook meat in butter, or add cream to a sauce or dish to serve with, or after, meat.

Slimmers

Roast meat, chicken or turkey are ideal. Duck and goose are high in calories. Salads, green vegetable dishes and desserts based on fruit are a wise choice. Dry wines are the best choice of alcohol.

Slimmers

One of your friends may be trying to lose weight, but if their diet is not too stringent they will probably eat most dishes you provide and balance their intake of food next day. If, however, your guest is serious in his or her intent to diet, then help as much as possible by a considerate choice of food. Avoid discussing diets if possible; they are horribly boring for the rest of the guests. Special menus are on pages 52 and 54.

Teetotallers

Make certain you have chilled tomato juice, apple juice and orange juice available together with drinks such as tonic water and bitter lemon. Try mixing orange and pineapple juice; a little grapefruit or orange juice with tomato juice, etc.

Teetotallers

If a guest says he or she does not drink alcohol, do not in any circumstances try to persuade them to change their mind. Serve non-alcoholic drinks without any comment. If you know in advance that your guest does not drink alcohol prepare a jug of iced fruit juice and decorate this with sliced orange and sprigs of mint. Frost the rim of the glass to make it look pretty. Brush this with a very little unbeaten egg white, then dip in caster sugar. In other words, take as much trouble with non-alcoholic drinks as with alcohol.

Guests on Special Diets

Diabetics
The people who suffer from diabetes are generally completely in control of their food intake and know exactly what they should, and should not, eat. You may well find that they can eat everything you suggest for the menu.

Fat-free Diets
A difficult menu to plan, but quite possible. You must make every effort to help your guest since this diet has to be followed without deviation. Wrap meat and fish in foil, moisten with wine or tomato purée, cook in wrapped parcels. Serve sorbets or other fruit desserts.

Gastric or Duodenal Ulcers
Even one meal badly selected can bring on discomfort or even severe pain. Allow plenty of time for a leisurely meal as rushed meals add to the problems of these people. Your guests may need to avoid alcohol. Modern drugs have helped to minimise strict dieting, but the points on the right are still important.

Emergency Measures

The notes given above and on page 38 presuppose you know in advance the special needs of your guests. There may, however, be occasions when you are told only about these at the last minute, after the meal has been planned and prepared. It is wise, therefore, to have 'stand-by' dishes or foods that can be offered. Naturally, owners of well-stocked freezers will find this less of a problem, so the suggestions below are based upon very simple foods that most people will have available, and the ideas given are for dishes that take minutes only to prepare.

Use eggs for scrambled eggs, omelettes or other savoury dishes. If you use 2-3 eggs per person the dishes are sufficiently sustaining to serve as a main dish. There are a number of egg dishes throughout the book which you will find indexed. Fortunately, eggs are acceptable on most diets, just adjust the method of cooking. The speedy dishes on pages 110 and 111 may be helpful.

Have additional vegetables available to make quick salads for slimmers; be prepared to sieve or liquidise the vegetables and mince the meat if someone is on a strict diet for an ulcer.

Fresh fruit can be made into a speedy fruit salad if any of your guests cannot eat rich, creamy desserts. Obviously the fruit salad is more interesting with cream as an accompaniment but this is a forbidden luxury for anyone on a fat-free diet. The simple recipe below is a good alternative.

Fat-Free 'Cream'

Warm the golden syrup. Whisk the egg white until stiff, then gradually whisk in the syrup.

Helpful Hints

Diabetics
This is the one occasion when it would be sensible to check the suggested menu with your guest if that is possible.

Fat-free Diets
Remember all foods must be cooked without fat and exclude egg yolks (whites are quite permissible) and cream; use skimmed milk.

Gastric
Avoid any highly spiced foods; it is wiser to serve fish dishes, creamed vegetables and milk type puddings, such as Crème Caramel, page 107.

Emergency Foods

Fruit juices, canned and/or fresh grapefruit for hors d'oeuvre.
Eggs for quick hors d'oeuvre or main dishes.
A selection of cheeses to give a protein food for vegetarians.
Fresh, canned and frozen vegetables.
Fresh and canned fruit.

Fat-Free 'Cream'

Serves 1-2
1tbspn golden syrup
1 egg white

The Hostess

My use of the word Hostess given with a capital 'H' throughout this book, as opposed to hostess (meaning the lady who is dealing with the entertaining), refers to the range of electrically heated trolleys, cabinets and trays manufactured by Ekco Heating & Appliances, Hastings, Sussex.

The Hostess and Frozen Foods

Never take a cooked meal or meat from the freezer and put this into any Hostess product to thaw out. The gentle heat of the appliance means ultra-long slow defrosting and harmful bacteria could develop. Never therefore use a Hostess product to re-heat foods. Use the oven or a saucepan, depending upon the kind of food, or use a microwave cooker.

Keeping Food Waiting

One of the problems you have when you entertain with little, if any, help in the kitchen, is to ensure that the prepared food is still in perfect condition when served to your guests. There are three alternative courses you can follow.

Firstly, you can plan the menu so that every dish is suitable for standing, or being left to cook, without any possibility of spoiling. Often, the advice given for an ideal meal when entertaining is — select a cold hors d'oeuvre or the kind of soup that cannot curdle or lose its texture, follow this with a cold, or casserole-type main dish, then a cold, or frozen, dessert. It is certainly possible to choose a number of dishes that come within this framework, but after a time your choice must become restricted, and you run the risk of repeating the same menus, or individual dishes, which can be boring for both the cook and the guests.

Secondly, you can select exactly the kind of dishes you prefer, without worrying about dishing-up ahead, and simply leave your guests while you serve the food. This procedure is fine if you entertain informally and do not mind leaving your guests, but has certain disadvantages. You cannot enjoy a leisurely, relaxed conversation before the meal; you must watch the clock and make quite certain the food is served immediately it is ready, otherwise there is the danger of it becoming dry, overcooked, or even spoiled. If you follow this procedure you also have the additional chore of washing dirty pots and pans at the end of the meal. There are few things more unpleasant-looking than a pile of dirty cooking utensils and these are more difficult to wash up after several hours than when freshly used. If you dish-up ahead, wash the pots and pans, so that later you only have to deal with the silver, china and glassware that have been used for serving and eating the food.

It can be extremely difficult to leave guests, particularly if you do not know them very well, while you spend time in the kitchen dishing-up. It generally means a poor husband has to deal single-handed with coats and cloakrooms for both sexes, introductions and drinks.

The third alternative is the one that has been used in this book; that is, to select those dishes which produce exactly the kind of menu you would prefer for each party — occasionally gloriously lavish and expensive, often practical and even economical — without worrying unduly about the problems of dishing-up. Why? Because you have learned the very best way of doing this so that hot food keeps really hot but fresh-looking, and cold dishes retain both texture and appearance.

There are only a very few dishes that need to be rushed on to the table the moment they are ready, the remainder can be dished up when it suits you, and before the guests arrive. This means you can wash up cooking utensils, have time to change and relax, welcome your guests and chat to them without fear of disasters in the kitchen.

Ham and Asparagus Rolls, Steak Kebabs and Hot Apricot Flan in a Hostess heated food cabinet (see page 50)

The Technique of Early Dishing-Up

The problems of keeping food in perfect condition vary, of course, according to the type of dish. Here are some general hints, but you will find specific types under each recipe.

The Problem

The Solution

Hors d'oeuvre
Pâtés dry very easily and seem to lack flavour if stored for too long in the refrigerator. Melon and grapefruit need chilling in the refrigerator but that seems to dry the cut surfaces.

Hors d'oeuvre
Keep well, but tightly covered, with clingfilm or foil until just before serving. Bring out of the refrigerator a short while before serving, as the pâté improves with being at room temperature for at least 30 minutes.

Not if clingfilm is placed over the plates or dish, but in such a way that it does not touch the flesh of the fruit. If it touches the fruit it absorbs some juice, which is a pity.

How to keep hot hors d'oeuvre looking as though they were freshly cooked.

As the information given throughout this book, under individual recipes. If the dishes have a crisp topping, do not cover, for condensation will spoil this; if they contain a sauce, cover tightly to keep the consistency perfect.

Soups and Sauces
To prevent mixture sticking or burning.

Soups and Sauces
Transfer the mixture to the top of a double saucepan over hot, but not boiling, water, or stand in a bain-marie, ie another container of very hot water, or pour or spoon into a hot tureen or sauce boat and cover tightly. Stand this in a Hostess trolley, or on a heat tray where the temperature is never so excessive that the mixture could spoil. You could also use one of the covered Hostess dishes, if more convenient. A cool oven is less good for soups and sauces. See Ways to Keep Food Waiting, pages 45-7.

To prevent a skin forming on the surface of the cooked soup or sauce.

Cover tightly as soon as the mixture is poured into the container; as an added precaution put either a few small pieces of butter or a damp piece of greaseproof paper over the surface of the soup or sauce, or hold back a little liquid, ie if the soup or sauce needs 600ml (1pt) liquid, use this *less* 2-3 tbspn. Pour the cooked soup or sauce into the heated dish, then pour the reserved cold liquid over the top, so excluding the air. Cover and keep hot; stir gently before serving so the extra butter or liquid is absorbed.

To avoid certain mixtures curdling in storage; this happens very easily if the dish contains egg, cream or wine.

Take particular care about the storage temperature. Hostess heated food trolleys and cabinets maintain a temperature of about 77°C (170°F) which is ideal. When cooking the soup or sauce make sure the mixture is not boiling when the egg, cream or wine is added, and do not return to the heat to cook further. Just dish-up and keep hot as recommended in the first paragraph under Soups and Sauces.

Fish Dishes
To prevent fish from tasting over-cooked.

Fish Dishes
Time the initial cooking carefully; if you plan to dish-up a considerable time ahead of the meal then under-cook by a minute or two. Try to serve fish dishes, though, within 30-40 minutes after cooking; fish is a food that deteriorates with standing.

The Solution

Coat with the appropriate sauce or a generous amount of melted butter. Cover if you want to keep the fish soft.

Prepare the sauce, etc, add the shellfish and continue cooking for a slightly shorter period than you would if serving the dish immediately, then transfer to the appropriate heated dish.

This depends upon the way in which the fish is fried. In Trout Meunière, for example, the fish does not become crisp and is simply placed on the heated dish, covered and kept hot (see page 75).

Batter-cooked fried foods do not keep particularly crisp and are better freshly served. If coated in egg and breadcrumbs, it can be kept hot successfully. Lift the cooked and well-drained fish on to absorbent paper on a large, flat dish. Do not cover, or allow the portions to touch and so cause condensation. Place in a low oven, the hot cupboard of a Hostess trolley or cabinet, or on a heat tray.

Meat and Poultry Dishes
Time the cooking carefully; under-cook rare beef by 1-2 minutes per 450g (1lb) and lamb if you like it 'pink', French-style, if you plan to dish-up well ahead of time. Make certain the serving dish is hot. Cover the joints if you want the outside to remain soft; leave uncovered if you prefer this crisp. Keep in a low oven, or the hot cupboard of a Hostess trolley or cabinet, or on a heat tray or in a bain-marie (the latter is not suitable where you have a crisp outside). You can carve the joint or poultry and then arrange it on a heated dish; on the whole if using this method it is advisable to cover the meat or poultry.

The gravy, stuffing and sauces may be dished up as the information given under Soups and Sauces (page 42), or in the individual recipes.

Follow the instructions given above under joints, or under fried and grilled fish above.

Dish-up earlier, providing you can keep the food at the ideal temperature, as in one of the Hostess dishes or your own tightly-covered casserole, on a heat tray or in a low oven or a bain-marie. Do not exceed approximately 77°C (170°F) — the temperature maintained in the Hostess trolley or cabinet — for the storage period. This temperature allows a good blending of flavours without fear of over-cooking or drying.

Vegetable Dishes
If you plan to keep vegetables hot for some time before the meal, under-cook by 1-2 minutes. Toss them in melted butter or margarine if they are not coated with a sauce. Always cover the container tightly to retain the moisture. A Hostess dish is ideal for keeping vegetables hot, or use your own flat-bottomed dishes on a heat tray, or use a bain-marie. The oven is not good for green vegetables as the dry heat tends to spoil colour and texture.
Never cover these. Arrange roast vegetables on a very hot dish and place in the hot cupboard of the Hostess trolley or cabinet, on a heat

The Problem

To prevent fish from becoming dry after being baked, grilled or fried without a coating.
To keep shellfish dishes hot for a period without toughening the fish.

To keep fried fish crisp until ready to serve.

Meat and Poultry Dishes
To keep a roast joint hot successfully.

How to keep grilled and fried meat pleasantly moist.

How to make sure a stew or casserole does not spoil by being over-cooked, or the liquid becoming too thick by prolonged evaporation.

Vegetable Dishes
How to keep green vegetables hot without losing their flavour and colour.

How to keep roast or fried vegetables crisp.

tray, or in a very low oven, making sure to have one layer only.

Fried vegetables should be spread over absorbent paper on a hot dish; never pile these high, just have a single layer so that you avoid condensation. Keep hot as for roast vegetables. A bain-marie is unsuitable for roast or fried vegetables.

Rice or Pasta Dishes
Cook as recommended in the recipe, time the cooking with particular care; drain and rinse the rice or pasta in boiling water, drain again, and then toss in a little hot oil or melted butter or margarine, or blend with the particular sauce. Put into a heated dish and cover.

Salads
Prepare and mix the salad. Put into the salad bowl or serving dish, cover tightly with foil or clingfilm and store in the refrigerator. Never add the oil and vinegar dressing until just before serving. The dressing can be made earlier and kept in a screw-topped jar; shake and add to the salad at the last minute. If the dressing is put on too early the salad looks limp and tired.

Pastry, Puddings and Desserts
The solutions are given in the individual recipes.

Croûtons and Toast
Fried bread, whether in large pieces or smaller shapes, known as croûtons, keeps hot very satisfactorily. Fry in hot oil, fat or butter, drain on absorbent paper for a minute, then transfer to a fresh flat dish covered with an absorbent doyley or paper, and stand inside a Hostess trolley or cabinet, on a heat tray, or in a low oven. Never cover fried bread.

Toast is a difficult food to keep hot; whatever you do it tends to become soggy, so it is better to make this at the last minute. If you have an electric toaster cut the bread, put on a plate, cover with foil, clingfilm or a table napkin until ready to toast.

Ways to Keep Food Waiting
On the following pages and under individual recipes, you will find advice on keeping food hot — or cold — as the case may be. The methods suggested are:

A cool oven: This is fairly satisfactory for keeping some foods hot for a limited period before the meal, but tends to have a drying effect if the food is retained in the oven for a prolonged period. The oven is not a good place for keeping cooked green vegetables, creamy soups and sauces; the former lose colour, the latter tend to spoil in texture. If the oven has not been used for baking or roasting, remember to pre-heat this for 15-20 minutes before the food is dished-up; set the thermostat to 110-120°C, 225-250°F, Gas Mark ¼-½, or as recommended by the manufacturer for the purpose of keeping food hot. If the oven has been used at a higher setting then leave the oven door open for a few minutes as you dish-up the food, to allow the temperature to drop. Do not forget to re-set the thermostat to the setting suggested above.

Rice or Pasta Dishes
How to prevent these dishes becoming sticky

Salads
To keep the salad looking fresh

Pastry, Puddings and Desserts
The problems vary according to the particular dish.
Croûtons and Toast
How do you keep these crisp?

Professional Touches
The finishing touches should add eye-appeal (a very important part of cooking good and appetising food) as well as increasing the flavour of the prepared dish.
Some garnishes or decorations must be added at the very last minute, so they retain their texture and appearance; others are improved by being put on to the food when it is dished-up, then kept warm in one of the ways suggested on pages 45-47.

(opposite) Fish Pancakes, Stuffed Crown Roast of Lamb and Lemon Apple Amber in a Hostess Sovereign trolley (see page 48)

Soups

Consider the colour, as well as the taste, of the cooked soup. Top rich, dark meat soups with cool-looking yoghurt, cream or soured cream, then chopped parsley or paprika.

If you add the yoghurt or cream when the soup is put into the serving dish it becomes warm if the soup is kept hot; but if you prefer the contrast of piping hot soup and cool yoghurt or cream, spoon this on the soup at the last minute.

Creamy soups need something bright or dark, such as blanched, then toasted, almonds, or chopped raw or canned red pepper.

Vegetable soups generally have plenty of natural colour so select a garnish that provides a pleasing contrast to the particular vegetables in the soup, such as chopped fresh parsley, chives or borage. Another interesting topping is grated cheese or tiny balls of cream cheese. The cheese is better added immediately before serving the soup.

Do not add crisp toasted or fried croûtons to the soup while it is being kept hot; these would soften and spoil. See page 44.

Fish

There are many garnishes that enhance fish, such as wedges or slices of lemon or orange (more original than lemon), chopped herbs, such as dill, fennel or parsley. These taste more mellow if kept hot for a time. Lemon or orange need not be added until the fish is on the point of being served; just prepare the fruit ready to put on the fish at the last minute, though the gentle warmth used to keep the food hot tends to improve the flavour of citrus fruit.

Many modern cookers, including the solid-fuel types, have two ovens, so you could use one at a low heat for keeping the food and plates hot.

A bain-marie: This is the cookery term used to describe the utensil of hot water in which certain foods, eg pâtés and dishes based upon egg custard, are cooked. The purpose is to prevent the outside of the food becoming dry and to assist in preventing the mixture reaching too high a temperature and so curdling. A bain-marie can also be used to keep cooked foods hot without spoiling. Use a large and fairly deep tin; half fill this with hot water. Dish-up the food into heat-resistant serving dishes, stand these in the bain-marie and place this over a low heat on top of the cooker or in a cool oven.

The disadvantage of using a bain-marie on top of the cooker is that the water creates a certain amount of steam in the kitchen unless you cover the tin with a lid or piece of foil. Obviously, while one can use this method of keeping soft foods hot, it is not successful where you want to keep a dry topping on the food, so cannot be used for pastry, crisp-skinned poultry, etc. Always make sure the water in the bain-marie is below boiling point so there is no fear of it bubbling in the tin and entering the containers of food.

Neither the oven nor the bain-marie provide the ideal answer to dishing-up ahead; you still need to bring the food from the kitchen into the dining room at the last minute, then dish-up each course separately.

The following appliances have been designed especially for the purpose of keeping cooked food hot. They enable you to dish-up as, and when, it is convenient to you. The temperatures of the Hostess heated trolleys, cabinets and heat trays are such that the food does not continue cooking, but stays looking and tasting freshly cooked for up to 2 hours before the meal is served. Switch on the appliance to pre-heat about 20 minutes before it is needed and leave it switched on.

A Hostess trolley is designed to keep a range of dishes hot. In the model shown in the colour picture on page 2 there are four oven-proof dishes with stainless steel lids. These are ideal for soups, dips, vegetables and mixtures coated with a sauce. Food can be cooked in the oven in these dishes if desired but the lids should not be put in the oven; cover the dishes with foil, or leave uncovered, depending upon the recipe. This model has a compartment below (known as the hot cupboard) with two heated shelves. These give enough space for large roasted joints or poultry, roasted vegetables, sauces, pies and desserts, plus room to warm the plates.

On page 93 the Hostess trolley shown has the four oven-proof dishes, one heated shelf and an extra space for warming the plates. The bottom shelf is not heated, so can be used for cold desserts, fruit, your coffee cups, etc.

The third variation of the Hostess trolley is illustrated on page 44; this has similar cupboard space with one heated and one unheated shelf. The flat top surface is heated and enables you to use your own serving dishes. It is better if these have flat bases for good contact. When you need a moist heat, place a lid on the dishes.

One popular way of using a Hostess trolley which offsets spillage if there are uneven surfaces (or steps) between the kitchen and dining room is to keep the trolley in the latter. Plug it into the mains to pre-heat about 20 minutes before you need it, then dish-up and carry the food through to the trolley in the serving dishes. Alternatively, pre-heat the Hostess trolley in the kitchen and load it as the food is cooked. Then carefully wheel the trolley into the dining room, plug in and leave it until you are ready to serve the meal. Keep the trolley closed up to keep in the heat. When serving, dishes are best left in the trolley, which is moved around so everyone can help themselves. You can remove the joint on to the table to carve, but leave the vegetables in their dishes in the trolley to keep them really hot.

There are now three variations of the Hostess heated food cabinet. The 'Sideboard' model (page 53) has four oven-proof dishes, the 'Cabinet Heat Tray' (page 41) has a heated flat stainless steel top on which you use your own dishes, and the 'Twin Casserole' cabinet (not illustrated) has two 2.8 litre (5pt) casserole dishes with lids. In each case there is a heated cupboard below. Most people like to place these cabinets on the sideboard or an adjacent shelf. The dishes can be put on to the table when the meal is served, but it is preferable for guests to help themselves from the cabinet. A recently introduced Hostess appliance is the 'Carousel'. This is a compact and attractive container for hot food as you will see from the picture on page 97. As the name suggests, the dish rotates so that guests can help themselves from the different sections if the 'Carousel' is placed in the middle of the table. Another new Hostess food server, the Hotpot Heat Tray, is shown on page 121. The 1.7 litres (3pt) casserole dish supplied is used to keep food hot, and the tray also warms the plates.

Hostess Heat Trays vary in size and finish, but enable you to put the dishes on top of the pre-heated surface and keep them there until everyone is ready for the meal (page 19). You may like to keep the heat tray on the sideboard or place it on a table. Always return the food to the Hostess appliance when everyone has been served so this keeps hot for second helpings.

Practical Serving Dishes

Remember that the dishes used to keep food hot for any length of time must be of the type recommended for this purpose. Dinner services today are generally made with the kind of serving dishes and plates that can be pre-heated quite satisfactorily, but always check on this point when shopping for china.

There are a great variety of 'cook-and-serve' dishes available and the terms used to describe these can be a little confusing. 'Heat-resistant' is a general term but means the food can be kept hot in the dish for a prolonged period. 'Oven-proof' means you can cook food in the dishes, but only in the oven. 'Flame-proof' on the other hand means the container can safely be used on top of the cooker, under the grill, or in the oven. Flame-proof dishes have another advantage in that they can be placed in a freezer, removed from this and then put straight into the cooker to reheat the food. You cannot do this, of course, with an oven-proof dish; after this has been in the freezer the food must be allowed to defrost at room temperature and the dish must also reach this temperature before it is safe to place it in the oven.

Fleurons (tiny shapes of baked puff pastry) make an excellent contrast to soft creamy fish dishes. These must be kept uncovered in the hot cupboard of a Hostess trolley or cabinet, or a cool oven so they retain their crisp texture.

Meat and Poultry
The stuffing or sauce or other accompaniments suggested in the recipes can be used as the garnish in many dishes. If you feel the finished dish lacks colour, then garnish it with rings of red and green pepper or water lilies of tomato. Watercress, lettuce and other crisp ingredients must be added when serving the food, but chopped fresh herbs have a pleasantly mellow flavour and retain their colour if kept in the gentle heat recommended.

Vegetables
Top creamed potatoes with small pieces of butter when you put these into the hot serving dish; then cover tightly. When you serve the potatoes the melted butter will have added richness to the smooth vegetable purée. For colour, add paprika, chopped parsley or chives.
Creamed or cooked spinach, sliced carrots, diced turnips or celeriac taste immeasurably better if you spoon a little double cream over the cooked vegetables before covering the dish. Cooked Brussels sprouts, cauliflower and broccoli can be topped with sauce, see pages 79 and 96. Another interesting but simple garnish is blanched, flaked almonds. Toss these in hot butter until golden brown.

Hot Puddings and Desserts
The decorations will vary a great deal, according to the particular dish. Fruit pies look more interesting if the pastry is dusted with sieved icing or caster sugar before serving.

6 Planning the Menu

Freezing and Shopping Ahead

The following recipes freeze well:

Fish Pancakes

Stuffed Crown Roast (ready to be cooked, defrost before cooking)

Lemon Apple Amber

Buy the fish for the filling or use frozen fish. A perfect cauliflower looks impressive and you can cook it whole. Keep well covered until ready to serve to prevent drying

On this and the following pages you will find a selection of menus. These are planned to give a balance of flavours and to be relatively easy for the hostess to prepare, cook and serve. You will note the short hints on working order, shopping, etc. These may prove a useful guide for the less experienced.

A choice of wines is given, on the left classic wines, on the right cheaper, but still appropriate, wines.

In one menu the cheese is placed before the dessert, French fashion. This seemed a wise procedure after the particular main course; you could, of course, serve it last, as is usual in Britain.

Dinner Party Menu 1

For Luxury	FISH PANCAKES	*For Economy*
Maçon Blanc		Italian Riesling
Beaune	STUFFED CROWN ROAST OF LAMB	Côtes du Rhône
Asti Spumante	CAULIFLOWER – BRUSSELS SPROUTS	Rouge
Madeira (Bual)	ROAST AND CREAMED POTATOES	

LEMON APPLE AMBER

CHEESE

Cook the dessert ahead to serve cold. Select the stuffing (those with fruit are excellent with lamb, see page 78), put into the crown, protect the ends of the bones with foil and roast. Cook the pancakes and the filling, put together, garnish with lemon and prawns, as in the picture on the left. Keep warm. Cook the vegetables, make the gravy. Dish up the food as it is cooked. See pages 110, 78, 91 and below for recipes, and colour picture on page 44.

Lemon Apple Amber

Serves 6

50g (2oz) sponge cake

1 small lemon

2 eggs

175g (6oz) caster sugar

600ml (1pt) thick unsweetened apple purée

3 tbspn lemon curd

Lemon Apple Amber

Make fine crumbs from the sponge, grate the top 'zest' from the lemon, squeeze out the juice, separate the eggs. Add the crumbs, lemon rind and juice, egg yolks and 50g (2oz) sugar to the apple purée. Put into a flan dish and bake in the centre of a cool oven, 150°C, 300°F, Gas Mark 2 for 1 hour. Spread with the lemon curd. Whisk the egg whites until stiff, fold in the remaining sugar. Spoon over the apple mixture, crisp in a very cool oven, 120-140°C, 250-275°F, Gas Mark ½-1 for 1-1¼ hours or in the Hostess hot cupboard as explained on page 107.

(opposite) Frikadeller and Caramelised Potatoes and Carrots (see pages 54 and 95)

48

Freezing and Shopping Ahead

The working plan on the right assumes none of the dishes are frozen ahead. Obviously, if you can do this it is a great help.
Foods that freeze well:
Consommé
Cherry sauce
Crème Brûlée (without the topping)
If using frozen duckling allow 24 hours for defrosting in the refrigerator. If fresh cherries are available use these for the sauce. It improves by standing for at least 24 hours.
Buy the artichokes

Dinner Party Menu 2

For Luxury	GLOBE ARTICHOKES WITH VINAIGRETTE	For Economy
Tio Pepe	DRESSING	Fino Amontillado
Chablis or Pouilly		Soave, or omit a
Fuissé	CONSOMMÉ	white wine and
Pommard★ or		serve a red
Château	ROAST DUCKLING WITH CHERRY SAUCE	Rioja
Giscours	GREEN PEAS – NEW POTATOES	Tinto★
(Margaux)★	GREEN SALAD	
Sancerre		
Liqueurs	CHEESES	
	CRÊME BRÛLÉE	

Although I believe duckling generally demands the freshness of white wine, in this case the Cherry Sauce dictates a more robust wine, so serve the white wine with the clear soup, have a red wine with the duckling and cheese, then return to the crisp, clear flavour of a Loire wine with the dessert.

Cook the custard base for the dessert; cook the artichokes. Make the consommé; then prepare the sauce and vegetables. Put the topping on the dessert and grill this. Roast the duckling(s) and cook the vegetables. Heat the consommé. Dish up the food as advised under the recipes. See pages 62, 64, 92 and 107 for recipes.

Freezing and Shopping Ahead

The following could be prepared and frozen:
Ham and Asparagus Rolls
Hollandaise sauce (freeze separately as it must be whisked again when reheating)
Meat on skewers for Kebabs with mushrooms but not tomatoes, onions or pepper
Flan case, but not the filled flan
If fresh apricots are available cook these, as they have more flavour than canned

Dinner Party Menu 3

For Luxury	HAM AND ASPARAGUS ROLLS	For Economy
Sancerre or dry		Valpolicella
Madeira	STEAK KEBABS	Lamberti
(Sercial)		
Volney	RICE-GREEN SALAD	
Apricot brandy		
	HOT APRICOT FLAN	

Make, or make and bake, the flan case, ready to reheat. Prepare the fruit filling; do not put into the pastry case until just before the meal. Prepare the salad and cover.

Ham and Asparagus Rolls: Heat thin slices of ham in a little stock, heat canned asparagus or cook the fresh vegetable, drain, put on to the slices of ham, roll. Put on to a hot dish and top with Hollandaise sauce, keep hot. Cook the rice, keep hot.

Steak Kebabs: Simmer small peeled onions in a little stock until tender, but unbroken, drain well. Put on skewers, with diced raw fillet or rump steak, small tomatoes, mushrooms and diced green pepper. Brush with oil, blended with a little salt and pepper, grill until tender. Dish up on the rice. Keep hot for a limited time. See page 109 for recipe for Apricot Flan, and colour picture on page 41.

50

Christmas
Luncheon or Dinner

For Luxury

Champagne
Gevrey
   Chambertin
Sauternes
Port or brandy

SMOKED SALMON CORNETS

ROAST TURKEY WITH STUFFINGS
AND ACCOMPANIMENTS
BREAD AND CRANBERRY SAUCES
ROAST POTATOES – BRUSSELS SPROUTS
SWEETCORN – GREEN PEAS

CHRISTMAS PUDDING
HARD SAUCE
BRANDY CREAM SAUCE

MINCE PIES

CHEESE
FRUIT AND NUTS

For Economy

Kriter
Châteauneuf du
   Pape

Freezing and Shopping Ahead

Much of the food for this menu can be frozen ahead:
Smoked Salmon Pâté
Stuffings
Bread and Cranberry Sauces
Mince Pies (cooked or
   uncooked)
Remember a large frozen turkey needs 72 hours to defrost in a refrigerator or 30 hours at room temperature, so purchase this at the right time. The moment it has defrosted it is highly perishable. Cranberries become scarce towards Christmas so buy early. Purchase vegetables in good time and store in a cool place

Prepare the Hard Sauce a day or so beforehand. Bake the Mince Pies, prepare the stuffings, sauces, Smoked Salmon Pâté and simmer the giblets on Christmas Eve. Put the stuffings into the turkey.

On Christmas Day put the turkey into the oven; place the Christmas Pudding on the cooker to steam. Spread the pâté (method below) to make the cornets; cook the vegetables, gravy and other accompaniments. Make the Brandy Cream Sauce, heat the Bread Sauce.

Dish up the food when ready and keep hot as advised under the recipes. See index and below for recipes; colour picture page 2.

Smoked Salmon Cornets: Spread the pâté over thin slices of smoked salmon, form into cornet shapes; garnish with lemon.

Hard Sauce (Brandy Butter)

Cream the butter until white. Sieve the icing sugar. Gradually beat into the butter, then add the brandy slowly and carefully. The mixture may be a little over-soft at this stage, so chill for a time, then pipe or pile into a pyramid shape. Decorate with small pieces of cherry and angelica. Chill well for at least 24 hours. Keep in the refrigerator until ready to serve. When quite firm cover lightly with clingfilm.

To freeze ahead
Do not freeze this.

Hard Sauce (Brandy Butter)

Serves 8-10
175g (6oz) unsalted butter
225g (8oz) icing sugar
3 tbspn brandy

To decorate
few glacé or Maraschino
   cherries
little angelica

Brandy Cream Sauce

Put the eggs and sugar into a basin over hot, but not boiling, water. Whisk until thick and creamy. Add the cream and brandy and whisk until thickened once again, serve pleasantly warm. This sauce should not be kept too hot. If made just before the meal it will be the right temperature if kept over warm water.

To freeze ahead
Do not freeze.

Brandy Cream Sauce

Serves 8-10
3 large eggs
75g (3oz) caster sugar
150ml (¼pt) double cream
brandy to taste

Freezing and Shopping Ahead

This is a simple menu but the following could be frozen:
Gazpacho (not
   accompaniments)
Buy fresh plaice or use frozen fish
Select an interesting variety of fresh fruits

Luncheon Party Menu 1

For Luxury	GAZPACHO	*For Economy*
Torres Viña Sol		Liebfraumilch
Tavel Rosé or	PLAICE GOUGÈRE	Blue Nun
Spanish De	BROCCOLI	
Casa Rosado		
	FRESH FRUIT SALAD	

This is a good luncheon for anyone who is slimming. Make the soup so it has time to become really cold. Prepare the fresh fruit salad. Make an orange-flavoured syrup, sweeten with sugar substitute if necessary, add seasonal fresh fruits. Make the Gougère; time the cooking so it is ready to serve as soon as cooked. Cook the broccoli and keep hot. See pages 73 and 77 for recipes and colour picture on page 76.

Freezing and Shopping Ahead

This menu is really so simple that freezing ahead is not necessary. The bacon and sauce are better if not frozen after cooking, although a frozen bacon joint could be used.
Pipe the Duchesse Potatoes on to a flat container, then freeze. Defrost and heat in the oven. The Chocolate Mousse should not be frozen unless adding the cream

Luncheon Party Menu 2

For Luxury	MELON	*For Economy*
White Port or an		Dry Cider
Amontillado	BACON WITH MARINADE SAUCE	
Vouvray	DUCHESSE POTATOES	
Tia Maria	COURGETTES OR CUCUMBER	
	CHOCOLATE MOUSSE	

Marinate the bacon for 24 hours as described in the recipe on page 94. Prepare the Chocolate Mousse, as the recipe below. Cook the potatoes, make the Duchesse Potatoes, pipe on to an oven-proof dish. Cook the bacon and make the sauce. Slice and simmer the courgettes or cucumber in boiling salted water, strain and toss in a little melted butter. Heat the Duchesse Potatoes. Keep all the food hot when cooked. See pages 94, 59, 96 for recipes and colour picture on page 81.

Chocolate Mousse: Separate the yolks from the whites of 4 eggs. Put the yolks into a basin together with 225g (8oz) plain chocolate. Heat over a pan of boiling water until the chocolate has melted, then stir briskly to blend. Add a little sugar if desired. Allow to cool and begin to stiffen slightly, then fold in the 4 stiffly whisked egg whites. Spoon into glasses and top with whipped cream.

This recipe can be varied in many ways. Add approximately 150ml (¼pt) whipped cream to the cool chocolate mixture, or add the finely grated rind of 2 oranges (use just the top 'zest') and 2tbspn Curaçao to the egg yolks and chocolate before melting, or add 1-2tbspn strong coffee, or the coffee liqueur Tia Maria or Kahlua, to the egg yolks and chocolate.

Large Mince Tart

If you like a generous amount of mincemeat in relation to pastry you will be well advised to make a large mince tart, rather than a number of small mince pies.

To make a 23-25cm/9-10in tart use about 450g (1lb) mincemeat, recipe as page 102, and flan (fleur pastry) made with 350g (12oz) flour, page 109. Instead of the richer pastry you could use shortcrust pastry made with 350g (12oz)flour, pinch salt, 175g (6oz) fat with cold water, or an egg yolk plus a little cold water, to bind. Shortcrust pastry does not produce the crisp sweet pastry that blends so well with mincemeat.

Roll out the pastry, use just over half to line the plate, dish or tin. Spoon the mincemeat over the pastry. Keep this away from the edges, so there is no possibility of the fruit mixture bubbling out during cooking. Moisten the edges of the pastry with a little cold water. Roll out the remaining pastry to a round sufficiently large to cover the mincemeat; seal the edges and flute, as shown in the picture above. If using flan pastry bake for approximately 30 minutes in the centre of a moderately hot oven, 190-200°C, 375-400°F, Gas Mark 5-6, reducing the heat slightly after 20 minutes. If using shortcrust pastry you can have a slightly hotter oven.

Turkey à la King, vegetables and a large Mince Tart in a Hostess heated food cabinet (see pages 87 and 102)

New Fillings

Mincemeat combines with many other ingredients; use a little less mincemeat in the filling for the tart and try these suggestions.

Mix mincemeat with diced fresh, or well drained canned pineapple.

Top the mincemeat with thick apple purée or thinly sliced apple slices.

Add well drained canned mandarin oranges to the mincemeat.

Top the mincemeat with a generous layer of grated fresh or desiccated coconut.

Freezing and Shopping Ahead

The Fruit Sorbet can be frozen well ahead and so can the Devilled Crab
Make either a Vinaigrette Dressing for Les Crudités (be sparing with oil for slimmers) or Mayonnaise or one of the dips on page 58

Pissaladière

Serves 6-8
short crust pastry made with 175g (6oz) flour etc (see page 109)
1 egg yolk or 1tbspn melted butter

For the filling
6 large ripe tomatoes
3 Spanish onions
1 garlic clove
4tbspn oil
2tbspn tomato purée
½tspn chopped fresh or pinch dried tarragon
½tspn chopped fresh or pinch dried rosemary
2tbspn grated Parmesan cheese
1 can anchovy fillets
few black olives

Caramelised Potatoes

Serves 6-8
675g (1½lb) small new potatoes
25g (1oz) caster sugar
25g (1oz) butter

Variation
Cooked carrots can be coated in the same way

Luncheon Party Menu 3

For Luxury Chablis	LES CRUDITÉS DEVILLED CRAB BROCCOLI FRUIT SORBET	*For True Slimmers* Fresh unsweetened Orange or Grapefruit Juice

This is a menu designed for people who are trying to lose weight. Freeze the Sorbet (the fruit depends upon the season). Prepare the Devilled Crab, heat just before the meal. Prepare the Crudités and Dips. See pages 58, 75 and 104 for recipes.

Pissaladière

Roll out the pastry to 0.5cm (¼in) and line a 23cm (9in) flan tin or dish. Brush the pastry with the beaten egg yolk or the melted butter and bake 'blind' in centre of hot oven, 220°C, 425°F, Gas Mark 7, for 15 minutes to completely set the pastry; do not allow to brown. Meanwhile peel, de-seed and chop the tomatoes. Peel and slice the onions; chop the garlic. Heat half the oil in a pan and add the tomato purée, cook until a thick purée is formed, stirring occasionally. Fry the onions in nearly all the remaining oil with the herbs and garlic. Sprinkle the pastry case with the cheese, add the onions and cover with the tomato purée. Arrange the anchovies in a latticework on top of the filling; place an olive in the centre of each square. Brush with the last of the oil. Reduce the oven heat to moderate, 180-190°C, 350-375°F, Gas Mark 4-5, and bake the flan in the centre of the oven for a further 15 minutes or until the crust is golden.

To keep the food hot
Brush the top of the flan and olives with a few drops of extra oil; this keeps the pleasant shine on the olives and anchovies. Lift on to a heated serving dish. Keep in the Hostess hot cupboard or on the heat tray or in the oven, turned very low (in this case, it is advisable to lay a piece of foil lightly over the filling).

To freeze ahead
Open-freeze then cover. Use within 3 months. Defrost before reheating.

Caramelised Potatoes

Scrub the potatoes and boil gently in their skins. Drain and skin. Heat the sugar slowly in a deep frying pan until it just melts. Add the butter. Rinse the potatoes in cold water, drain and add to the sugar mixture. Heat gently until glazed and lightly browned. See colour picture on page 49.

To keep the food hot
These potatoes can burn easily, so dish up as soon as ready. Lay on to a flat dish, do not cover, and keep hot in the Hostess hot cupboard or on a heat tray or in a cool oven. Do not attempt to freeze.

Dishes for Buffet Parties

There are many recipes throughout this book that are suitable for buffet parties. Do not be too conservative in your choice of foods, have a mixture of hot and cold dishes when the weather is suitable. Advice on how to keep the foods hot without spoiling is given on pages 40 to 47.

Suprême of Fruit   Melon Cocktail
Avocado Dishes   Crudités
Smoked Salmon Pâté   Liver Pâté
Ratatouille   Mixed Vol-au-Vents
Fish Cocktails   Delhi Prawns
Quiche aux Champignons   Pissaladière

Any of the hot or cold soups in the book

Fish Salads   Trout with Dijon Sauce
Devilled Crab   Salmon Walewska

Selection of Cold Meats, including Salami
Turkey à la King   Turkey Stroganoff
Turkey and Walnut Croquettes   Crispy Chicken Salad
Party Meatballs and Sausages with Dips   Polynesian Beef
Frikadeller with Caramelised Potatoes
Spaghetti Bolognese   Paella
Meat Fondue   Cheese Fondue
Salads of all kinds

Any of the gâteaux or desserts in the book

Selection of cheeses

The recipes given above are all indexed. The choice of wines depends upon the foods selected; often a rosé wine is a good choice. For information on wines see pages 26 to 37.

Slimmers will prefer a buffet party menu, for they can select the dishes and portions that enable them to keep within their diets. Children and young people enjoy the informality of a buffet. Make sure you have sausages on sticks, potato crisps, ice cream on your menu for younger children. Older children generally enjoy spaghetti and rice dishes.

Outdoor Eating

There are many occasions when one can entertain guests out-of-doors. Food can be served on the patio, on the beach, at race meetings or when visiting beauty spots.

Modern insulated boxes and bags enable you to carry either hot or cold food. Follow the directions for chilling any attachments for these.

Obviously one cannot carry a mixture of hot and cold dishes in the one bag or box.

Make use, also, of wide-necked vacuum flasks for transporting hot or cold soups, food in sauces, fruit salads, etc. Use polythene bags or boxes to carry crisp salad ingredients.

It is helpful to bake quiches, tarts and similar foods in heavy foil dishes and leave them in the dishes to prevent any possibility of food breaking.

If you are serving food in the garden your menu can be quite elaborate and suitable dishes kept hot as advised in this book. Small children love the fun of a picnic, even if it takes place in the garden. Give them polythene disposable tumblers and picnic plates so breakages cannot occur.

7 Food for Parties

Delicious Dishes

The secret of perfection in cooking is to take time and trouble in choosing ingredients and method of cooking.
It is also essential to develop a discerning palate, so taste as you prepare the food, add flavourings and seasonings slowly and carefully.
Never over-flavour or over-season when cooking for other people. Tastes vary and it is better to allow your guests to add extra seasoning, if they so desire.

Party Meatballs

Makes 30-40 meatballs
1 small onion
1 tbspn oil
450g (1lb) raw minced beef
25g (1oz) fresh white
    breadcrumbs
1 tbspn Worcestershire sauce
salt and pepper
little flour

For frying
4-6 tbspn oil

To serve
cocktail sticks
Red Devil Dip or Barbecue
    Sauce (page 58)

On the following pages you will find many dishes for the various courses and types of meals, ranging from Appetisers and Hors d'oeuvre to the cheese course.

All the recipes suggested in the menus in the previous section are included, together with many others, so that you can build up a really extensive repertoire of food for enjoyable entertaining.

Appetisers

Small canapés take time to prepare; you may therefore find it easier, and more enjoyable, to prepare one or more sauces, or dips, and have meatballs, as the recipe below, or tiny cooked cocktail sausages or large prawns to serve with these. The picture on the right shows how inviting these can look.

If you have fairly satisfying appetisers you could omit the hors d'oeuvre or soup from the meal.

Party Meatballs

Peel and finely chop the onion. Heat 1 tbspn of oil in a saucepan, fry onion gently for 5 minutes or until soft. Blend with the minced beef, breadcrumbs, Worcestershire sauce, salt and pepper. Combine all the ingredients until thoroughly mixed. Pinch off small pieces, about the size of a walnut, and roll between floured hands to form small balls. Heat the oil in a large and fairly deep frying pan or shallow saucepan, add the meat balls. Fry gently until browned on all sides; this takes about 10 minutes. Turn meatballs with two spoons as they cook. Spear the meatballs with cocktail sticks and place on a large platter with a small bowl of the dip or sauce. See colour picture opposite.

To keep the food hot
Cook as the recipe, drain on absorbent paper, then reheat in a cool oven or put on a flat dish in the Hostess trolley, cabinet or on a heat tray.

To freeze ahead
Cook, cool; open-freeze, without cocktail sticks, then wrap. Use within 3 months.

(opposite) Party Meatballs and Barbecue Sauce (see above and page 58)

To make Vol-au-vents

These pastry cases can be 'bite-sized' to serve with drinks, or larger for an hors d'oeuvre or main course. Make puff pastry (page 83) or buy frozen puff pastry. Roll out until about ½-1cm (¼-½in) thick for tiny pastry cases, but rather thicker for larger cases. Remember, puff pastry rises dramatically and if you make tiny cases too deep they could 'topple-over' in baking. Cut out small rounds, put on a baking tray. Use a smaller cutter and press half way through the dough — see sketch.

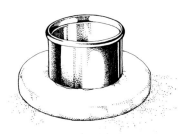

Bake the puff pastry as page 83; allow about 10 minutes for cocktail-sized rounds. When cold, gently remove the centre 'lid'. Dry out the pastry case, if necessary, for a few minutes in the oven.
Fill with flaked, minced or diced fish, poultry, game or cooked vegetables (such as mushrooms) in a thick sauce or mayonnaise. Remember, hot fillings must be placed into hot pastry just before serving.

Savoury Dips

The sauces below make good 'dips' for the Meatballs on page 56, for cooked sausages, large peeled prawns or crisp raw vegetables.

Other dips are made by blending sieved cottage cheese, or finely grated cheese with mayonnaise and/or yoghurt and various flavourings and ingredients such as Tabasco sauce, tomato ketchup, flaked crabmeat, canned tuna, avocado purée. Make the dip the consistency of a thick cream, spoon into a bowl and stand on a large dish or tray. Arrange potato crisps, small biscuits and a selection of vegetables around.

Barbecue Sauce
Serves 6
Peel and grate 1 medium onion. Heat 1tbspn oil in a saucepan and cook onion gently for 3 minutes. Add a 398g (15oz) can peeled tomatoes and 2-2½tbspn Worcestershire sauce. Cover the pan and simmer for 15 minutes, sieve or liquidise and return to the pan. Blend 2tspn cornflour with 2tbspn water, stir into sauce. Bring to the boil and cook until thickened. Add salt, pepper and approximately 2tspn brown sugar, or to taste. Serve hot or cold.

Red Devil Dip
Serves 6
Peel and finely chop about 4 sticks celery; peel and chop, or grate a large onion. Heat 2tbspn oil in a saucepan, fry the celery and onion for 5 minutes, or until soft. Add a 398g (15oz) can tomatoes, 3tbspn tomato ketchup, 2tbspn Worcestershire sauce with salt and pepper to taste. Simmer for 20 minutes, cool slightly. Sieve or liquidize to make a smooth purée. Serve hot or cold.

To keep the food hot
See Soups and Sauces, page 42.

To freeze ahead
Both sauces freeze well for 3 months.

Les Crudités
This is the name given by the French to a selection of crisp young vegetables, such as cauliflower florets, whole baby carrots or strips of larger carrots, diced celery, spring onions, wedges of cucumber or tomatoes, radishes, etc. The dips and sauces on this page make interesting accompaniments, or serve bowls of thick Mayonnaise or Vinaigrette Dressing.

Hors d'oeuvre

This course can change and turn a prosaic, or family, menu into a special occasion meal. An hors d'oeuvre precedes the soup or takes the place of soup in a shorter menu.

Fruit Juices and Fruit

Fruit juice is dull, but could be served for a light luncheon (see page 39). Fruit, on the other hand, gives good scope for ingenuity and, in most cases, can be prepared ahead.

Grapefruit and Avocado

Cut away the peel and pith from the whole grapefruit, skin and halve the avocados. Blend the fruits together and toss immediately in the lemon juice and oil; season well. Shred the lettuce finely, put this into individual glasses and top with the grapefruit mixture. Serve very cold.

This recipe can be made more interesting by the addition of 50-100g (2-4oz) peeled prawns, and you can use a Mary Rose Dressing (page 64) instead of the lemon juice and oil.

Jamaican Grapefruit

Soften the butter slightly. Halve the grapefruit, scoop out the pulp (retain the grapefruit shells), peel and slice the bananas. Blend with the rum, half the sugar and the raisins. Spoon back into the grapefruit cases. Spread the butter over the grapefruit mixture, sprinkle with the remaining sugar and put for a few minutes only under the grill until the sugar melts. Serve hot. The grapefruit cases can be filled ahead or the dish heated and kept warm.

Melon

Melon, when really perfect, is a delicious start to a meal. There are simple suggestions for serving it on page 14 but one of the most luxurious and simple dishes is to add slices of proscuitto (smoked Parma ham) to the fruit. Serve with brown bread and butter. Fresh figs or dessert pears are another excellent accompaniment to Parma, or other kinds of smoked ham.

Melon and Prawns

This hors d'oeuvre is less well known, but excellent. Arrange the shelled prawns on each plate beside the melon; top the fish only with mayonnaise; garnish with lemon. The melon needs to be ripe for the two dishes above so you do not need to add sugar.

Suprême of Fruit

The Americans make this delicious meal-starter, an assortment of fresh fruits served in tall glasses and well chilled. The fruit must be kept sharp in flavour and not over-sweetened so that the dish makes a refreshing start to the meal.

Grapefruit and Avocado

Serves 6-8
2 large grapefruit
2 large avocados
2 tbspn lemon juice
1 tbspn oil
salt and pepper
lettuce heart

Jamaican Grapefruit

Serves 8
40g (1½oz) butter
4 large grapefruit
4 medium bananas
2 tbspn rum
50g (2oz) brown sugar
50g (2oz) seedless raisins

Melon Accompaniments

Allow about 25g (1oz) ham or shelled prawns with each portion of melon. A good-sized cantaloup or less expensive honeydew melon can be cut into 4-6 portions. A medium charentais or ogen melon is halved for 2, and a small one served whole.

Avocados

This fruit has become very popular and is obtainable all the year round. It makes a good hors d'oeuvre, or part of a salad, providing everyone enjoys the unique flavour. Avocados darken in colour easily, so sprinkle with lemon juice.

Cucumber and Avocado Cream

Dice the cucumber and one avocado, sprinkle with some lemon juice, salt and pepper. Spoon into glasses. Peel and mash the second avocado with the rest of the lemon juice and ingredients, except a little yoghurt. Top with this and parsley. See colour picture opposite.

Avocado Vinaigrette

First make the Vinaigrette Dressing on page 64. You may, however, like to increase the proportion of lemon juice or vinegar to oil to give a sharper flavour. Halve each avocado, remove the stone, spoon dressing into the centre. Put a sauceboat of dressing on the table so that each person can add more if desired.

Avocados with Shellfish

Prepare the avocados as above. Fill the centre with shelled prawns, flaked crabmeat or diced lobster. Top with the Vinaigrette Dressing, Mayonnaise, or a Mary Rose Dressing (page 64).

Another version of this dish is to blend the shellfish with enough well-flavoured whipped cream, or a White, or Cheese Sauce, page 79, to bind. Spoon the mixture into the avocados, then brown under the grill; or top with breadcrumbs and grated cheese and serve 'au gratin'.

Cheese-filled Avocado

Blend the cream cheese, half the grated cheese, chopped herbs and capers together. Moisten with the cream, season well. Halve the avocados, remove the stones. Spoon the filling into each half and sprinkle the remaining cheese over the top. Brown under the grill. You could use 300ml (½pt) thick Cheese Sauce instead of cream cheese and cream. There are quite a number of variations you could make; for example add chopped nuts (a good dish then for vegetarians), or finely diced cooked ham or chopped shellfish. Flavour the mixture with a little curry paste or powder.
Note: Use a flame-proof dish when browning under the grill.

Fried Avocados with Herbs

This is delicious, but a difficult dish for a cook-cum-hostess, since the avocados must be prepared and fried at the last minute. If you can leave your guests or have help in the kitchen, try this. Blend the butter with one-third of the lemon juice, the herbs, salt and pepper. Cut into 8 portions and mould these into small squares and chill until hard. Pre-heat the pan of oil. Skin, then halve, the avocados. Put the firm herb-butter into each half. Insert tiny wooden cocktail sticks into four of the halves, then press the other halves on top so that the avocados look whole again. Sprinkle with remaining lemon juice; beat the egg, brush over the avocados, then roll in the breadcrumbs. Deep fry for 2-3 minutes only; serve at once.

Cucumber and Avocado Cream

½ cucumber
2 avocados
2tbspn lemon juice
salt and pepper
142ml (5 fl oz) soured cream or
    Mayonnaise
4-5tbspn yoghurt
parsley

Avocado Vinaigrette

Allow ½ an avocado and
1-2tbspn Vinaigrette Dressing
per person

Avocados with Shellfish

Allow approximately 40g
(1½oz) shellfish, ½ an avocado
per person and 2tbspn dressing

Cheese-filled Avocado

175g (6oz) cream cheese
4tbspn grated Parmesan cheese
1-2tspn chopped mixed herbs
1tspn capers
approximately 3 tbspn double
    cream
salt and pepper
3 large avocados

Fried Avocados with Herbs

Serves 4
75g (3oz) butter
3tbspn lemon juice
1tbspn chopped parsley
1tbspn chopped chives
salt and pepper
4 avocados

To coat
1 egg
50g (2oz) crisp breadcrumbs
    (raspings)

For deep frying
oil

(opposite) Cucumber and Avocado Cream

Vegetables as an Hors d'oeuvre

Asparagus and globe artichokes are eaten hot or cold, and page 43 describes the best way of keeping hot vegetables looking and tasting as though freshly cooked. You may need finger bowls (see page 14).

Asparagus

You need about 450g (1lb) for 2 large or 3 smaller portions. Serve hot with very hot seasoned butter (allow about 40g (1½oz) per person), or with Hollandaise or Mousseline Sauce, recipes on page 79. Serve cold asparagus with Vinaigrette Dressing, recipe page 64.

Asparagus

Good asparagus stems should be firm, not limp. Cut away the tough ends, scrape the white stems to clean, wash in cold water. Tie loosely in bundles, or stand upright in a deep basket (the kind used for blanching vegetables ready for freezing, is ideal). Place the asparagus in a pan of boiling salted water, cover with a lid, or use foil if there is no suitable lid. Cook steadily for 20-30 minutes, depending upon the thickness of the stems, until the tips and top of the stem are tender. Drain, serve hot or cold, as the suggestions on the left.

To eat asparagus, dip the tips in the hot butter, hot or cold sauce or dressing. Discard the tough part.

Globe Artichokes

You need one artichoke per person. Serve hot, as given under asparagus, above. If serving cold, fill centres with Vinaigrette Dressing, chopped prawns or other shellfish in Mayonnaise or inexpensive Danish 'caviar' or softly scrambled eggs.

Globe Artichokes

Globe artichokes should be green and firm; wrinkled brown tips indicate staleness. Cut away the stalks and any hard outer leaves; the inner 'choke' (centre part) may be cut away before cooking or pulled out after cooking. Sprinkle with a little lemon juice to keep the vegetable from darkening; an enamel-coated saucepan also helps. Cook in boiling salted water for 20-35 minutes, depending upon size. To test if cooked, pull away one outer leaf and see if the base is tender. Serve hot or cold as indicated left.

The leaves are pulled away and the tender base eaten with the fingers; discard the tough part of the leaves; but the base, the 'heart', is eaten with a knife and fork.

Ratatouille

Serves 8
3 onions
2-3 garlic cloves
675g (1½lb) tomatoes
5-6 medium courgettes
2 large aubergines
4tbspn olive oil
salt and pepper

To garnish
chopped parsley

Variation
Diced red and/or green peppers, also sliced mushrooms can be added if desired

Ratatouille

Peel and chop the onions, peel and crush the garlic, skin and chop the tomatoes. Wash, dry and slice or dice the courgettes and aubergines neatly; keep a uniform thickness. Heat the oil, add the onions and garlic, then the tomatoes. Cook slowly until the juice flows. Add the courgettes and aubergines, with salt and pepper to taste. Cover the pan, simmer gently for about 45 minutes or until all the vegetables are soft but unbroken. This can be done ahead and the vegetable mixture reheated. If more convenient, cook in a covered casserole in a very moderate oven for the same time. Top with chopped parsley. This is equally good served hot or cold, as an hors d'oeuvre or a vegetable dish.

To keep the food hot
Ratatouille seems to improve with being kept hot at a gentle heat. Use the covered Hostess dish (see pages 45-47) or a tightly covered vegetable dish on a heat tray or in a cool oven.

To freeze ahead
This freezes perfectly. Use within 1 year.

Fish

Many kinds of fish can be served for an hors d'oeuvre, the simplest being smoked fish, ie smoked salmon, eel, trout or mackerel, or try the less usual smoked sprats. Allow approximately 50g (2oz) smoked salmon or filleted eel per person. Allow slightly more if the eel is smoked on the bone. Allow a small smoked trout per person or 100g (4oz) smoked sprats. Mackerel are very large and filling, so serve neat portions weighing approximately 75-100g (3-4oz) as an hors d'oeuvre.

The accompaniments for smoked fish are simple; smoked salmon is served with lemon and cayenne pepper, the other fish listed above with horseradish cream and lemon. Garnish the fish with lettuce, and you could add one or two pieces of tomato or cucumber, but elaborate salads are not usual unless you decide to have the fish as a light main course. Serve with brown bread and butter.

The Scandinavians have a clever accompaniment to serve with all smoked fish. They prepare creamy scrambled egg, let this get firm, then cut into neat fingers and place these beside the fish on the plate. It not only makes expensive smoked fish more sustaining, but it is a pleasant contrast to the richness of the fish.

Fish Salads

Small portions of cooked fresh salmon, lobster or crab are an ideal start to the meal. Do not serve too large helpings, since they are very sustaining. Advice on preparing and serving these fish is given on page 74.

Sardines and Whitebait

Fresh sardines have become very popular, so if you have the facilities to keep the cooked fish hot, as described on page 43, fry or grill these in a little butter for 4-5 minutes, top with chopped herbs and lemon. Whitebait is coated with a little well-seasoned flour then deep fried in hot oil; sardines can be cooked in the same way. The fish must then be eaten at once. Serve with cayenne (the very hot) pepper, lemon and brown bread and butter. Cold sardines can be tossed in Vinaigrette Dressing, chopped herbs and topped with fresh tomato purée.

Horseradish Cream

Blend the cream and horseradish; as you do so the cream will thicken, then add the other ingredients, tasting as you do this.

To freeze ahead
Do not freeze.

Mixed Hors d'oeuvre

Serve the various ingredients on special dishes with divided compartments, or in individual containers so everyone can select their favourite foods. Include:
1 Various salads and vegetables.
2 Fish Cocktails, together with sardines, anchovy fillets, smoked fish and/or one of the fish dishes on pages 64, 66 and 74.
3 Egg Mayonnaise. Hard-boil eggs, shell and top with mayonnaise, then strips of smoked salmon, anchovies, or canned or fresh red peppers.
4 Hot or cold vol-au-vents (page 58).
5 Liver or fish pâtés (page 68).
6 Salami and/or other savoury sausage.
Make sure the assortment of ingredients is colourful as well as appetising.

Sardines and Whitebait

Allow 100g (4oz) fish per person. Wash, dry, but do not remove the heads.

Horseradish Cream

Serves 6-8
300ml (½pt) double cream
4-5tbspn finely grated fresh
    horseradish
1-2tbspn white vinegar or
    lemon juice
salt and pepper
good pinch sugar
little made English mustard

Fish Cocktails

Allow approximately 2tbspn Mayonnaise per person. To flavour this add:
  tomato ketchup or purée
  soy sauce
  Worcestershire sauce
  single or double cream
  little sherry or brandy.
Allow approximately:
  50g (2oz) shelled prawns, or crabmeat or lobster or cooked fish (fresh salmon, turbot, haddock, kipper fillet) per person.
Add:
  mushrooms and pepper
  celery and avocado
  grapefruit and avocado
  orange and celery
  melon and pepper.
Allow:
  2 or 3 lettuce leaves per person.
Mary Rose Dresssing: This is the name given to tomato-flavoured mayonnaise.

Shellfish

Allow about 6 very large prawns per person. Half a small to medium-sized lobster or small crab are generally enough for one person as an hors d'oeuvre. They can be served in the shell; page 74 gives details of serving. The recipe for Mayonnaise on the right would be enough for 6-8 people, although it is advisable to make too much rather than too little. This would keep in the refrigerator for up to 10 days, but do not freeze.
Vinaigrette Dressing keeps well, but it is better freshly made when adding chopped fresh herbs (parsley, chervil, tarragon, chives, etc).

Fish Cocktails

These are one of the easiest of all fish dishes to prepare, since everything is done ahead. The only problem about a fish cocktail is that it can be monotonous unless you use clever flavourings with the fish. The suggestions on this page should help to make the fish cocktails you prefer really interesting.

Prepare the dressing; add the extra ingredients to the Mayonnaise, recipe below; taste as you do so. You will not need all these, but use enough to make the sauce interesting.

If you decide to use some cooked fish as well as shellfish, blend this with some of the sauce while it is still warm, then allow to cool. In this way the fish will absorb more flavour from the dressing. Decide what other ingredients to add to the fish and dressing. Suggestions are given on the left; these are in pairs so that you have a combination of flavours. Do not use too many additions, otherwise the flavour of the cocktail becomes unbalanced. Prepare and dice these ingredients, blend with the fish mixture, chill well.

Shred the lettuce very finely; remember it is to be eaten with a teaspoon. Nothing is worse than trying to cope with lumps of lettuce. Put some into individual glasses, or on to attractive small plates. Top with the fish mixture, a little more dressing, and garnish with wedges of lemon. Serve with brown bread and butter.

Shellfish for Hors d'oeuvre

If you are certain all your guests like shellfish, then select it as an hors d'oeuvre. Details on preparing lobster and crab are given on pages 74 and 75, together with a recipe for Moules Marinière. Naturally you would give smaller portions than when serving it as a main course.

If you can obtain large Mediterranean prawns, serve these with Mayonnaise. Arrange the prawns on a dish (do not shell them) with a little lettuce and lemon to garnish. Obviously, other shellfish can be served in the same way or with a mixed salad, tossed in Vinaigrette Dressing. This can be made ahead and stored in an airtight jar.

Mayonnaise

Blend the yolks of 2 eggs with a little salt, pepper, pinch of sugar and mustard powder. Gradually blend in by hand, or in a liquidiser, up to 300ml (½pt) olive oil or good quality salad oil. Add slowly 1-2tbspn lemon juice or white wine vinegar and 1-2tbspn boiling water (optional).

Vinaigrette Dressing

Blend 1tbspn made mustard with a pinch of salt, pepper and sugar. Gradually work in up to 150ml (¼pt) olive, or salad, oil, then about 4tbspn red or white wine or malt vinegar. Adjust the seasoning and add chopped herbs, crushed garlic, etc to taste.

(opposite) Scalloped Salmon (see page 111)

Delhi Prawns

Serves 8
1 medium onion
1 large dessert apple
2-3 celery sticks, from the heart
50g (2oz) butter
1 tbspn curry powder
1 tspn cornflour
1 tspn tomato purée
300ml (½pt) single cream
salt and pepper
450g (1lb) shelled prawns

To serve
100-175g (4-6oz) long grain
    rice, cooked as method on
    page 114
chutney

Variations
1 To make a more economical
dish, use half cream and half
milk with 1½tspn cornflour
2 To give a greater variety of
texture, add 50g (2oz) flaked
blanched almonds or pine nuts
to the cooked sauce
3 This is an excellent cold dish;
blend 2-3tbspn Mayonnaise
with the sauce when it has
cooled

Trout Deauville

Serves 8
8 small fresh trout
100g (4oz) butter
salt and pepper
2 tbspn lemon juice
150ml (¼pt) dry white wine
4 tbspn chopped parsley
2 tbspn chopped chives
300ml (½pt) double cream
8 tbspn fine soft breadcrumbs

To garnish
2 lemons
2 tbspn chopped parsley

Variations
1 If the trout are large, use 4
only and cut these into 8 fillets
2 Use cider in place of wine
3 Use cutlets of salmon or
salmon trout in place of trout

Delhi Prawns

Peel the onion, chop very finely; peel, core and finely dice the apple and dice the celery. Heat the butter in a pan, toss the onion in this for several minutes until soft; add the apple, celery, curry powder, cornflour and tomato purée. Blend with the onion, then gradually stir in the cream. Bring the mixture to the boil, stirring all the time, add the salt, pepper and prawns. Heat for a few minutes only, as the apple and celery should retain a certain crispness. Serve on a bed of rice. Serve chutney separately.

To keep the food hot
Both the rice and the prawn mixture should be kept tightly covered to prevent drying. The food looks more interesting and is easier to serve if put on a fairly large flat dish, or you could use individual ramekin dishes. Keep hot as below.

To freeze ahead
The apple and celery tend to lose their crispness if the mixture is frozen, so prepare the dish without these, add when reheating after freezing. Use within 6 weeks.

Trout Deauville

Although the heads of trout are often left on the fish, it is advisable to remove these for this particular dish. Cut off the heads, split the fish, wash and dry. Melt the butter, put half on one side, but blend 50g (2oz) with a little salt and pepper, the lemon juice, wine and herbs. Place the trout in a large shallow oven-proof or flame-proof serving dish (use the latter if browning under a grill). Pour the butter mixture over the fish. Cover the dish with foil or a lid and bake the fish in the centre of a moderate oven, 190°C, 375°F, Gas Mark 5, for 15 minutes, or until the fish is just cooked. Meanwhile whip the cream until it just holds its shape, add a little salt, pepper, then the remaining melted butter and the breadcrumbs. Spread neatly over the fish, taking care that this topping does not drop into the wine liquid in the dish. Either place under a pre-heated grill or towards the top of a hot oven (the heat should be raised to 220°C, 425°F, Gas Mark 7) and leave for a few minutes to give a delicate brown colour to the topping. Halve the lemons, spoon out the pulp, sprinkle over the fish, then add the parsley.

To keep the food hot
This dish should be served as soon as possible after cooking, but can be kept hot for up to 30 minutes in the hot cupboard of a Hostess trolley or cabinet, on a heat tray or in a cool oven. Cover the dish with foil.

To freeze ahead
Frozen trout can be used for this dish. Defrost to remove the heads.

Pâtés

Do not regard a pâté simply as an hors d'oeuvre. You could plan a light luncheon around a selection of pâtés; serve with salad to make a more sustaining meal.

Liver and meat pâtés, whether home-made or bought, are doubly interesting if accompanied by Cumberland Sauce (recipe below).

Sometimes commercially-made pâtés are a little over-firm or strongly flavoured; you can give them a softer texture and more subtle flavour if you blend them with a little double cream or cream cheese.

In these days when many families have a liquidiser (blender) or food processor you can produce a pâté within minutes from cooked poultry, game or certain meats, such as ham. If you are using a liquidiser you must melt the butter, otherwise the mixture is too stiff for the appliance to handle. In a food processor, on the other hand, while you can use melted butter, you could, if in a hurry, add the butter straight from the refrigerator. Naturally, if the butter is melted you must allow the pâté to stand for at least two hours to set.

Speedy Pâté

If using raw liver, cook lightly in the butter; if using meat, melt the butter if necessary, but see comments above. Peel the garlic, dice the cooked poultry or meat. If using a liquidiser you will need to add the ingredients in batches, but you should be able to blend the ingredients at one time in the food processor.

Serve as Liver Pâté (page 68).

Cumberland Sauce

Halve the oranges, squeeze out the juice. Remove the peel from 1 orange, cut away any white pith from the peel, then slice the orange-coloured part ('zest') into matchstick pieces. Put these into a saucepan with the water; allow to stand for an hour if possible. Simmer gently for 15 minutes, or until the peel is just tender and the liquid reduced to 150ml (¼pt). Add the lemon juice and mustard. Blend the port wine with the arrowroot or cornflour (the former gives a clearer sauce) together with the jelly, salt and pepper to taste. Stir over a low heat until the mixture thickens, then allow to simmer gently until the desired consistency. Serve cold with pâté or hot with ham.

To freeze ahead
This can be frozen for 2 months if the port wine is omitted (it loses its potency). Add when defrosted and reheat.

Speedy Pâté

Serves 6-8
450-550g (1-1¼lb) calves' or
   lambs' liver; or cooked duck,
   game or ham
75g (3oz) butter
1-2 garlic cloves
4-6tbspn single cream
2tbspn sherry or brandy
salt and pepper

Cumberland Sauce

Serves 6-8
2 large oranges
300ml (½pt) water
1tbspn lemon juice
1-2tspn made English or
   French mustard
4tbspn port wine
1tspn arrowroot or cornflour
8tbspn redcurrant jelly
salt and pepper

67

Liver Pâté

Serves 10-12
1-2 garlic cloves
350g (12oz) lambs' or calves' liver
225g (8oz) pigs' liver
300g (10oz) belly of pork or fat bacon
sprig thyme
50g (2oz) butter
40g (1½oz) flour
150ml (¼pt) milk
6tbspn double cream
3tbspn sherry or brandy
3 eggs
salt and pepper
½-1tspn finely grated lemon rind (optional)

Variations
1. Line the tin with rashers of de-rinded streaky bacon, fill with pâté mixture, top with more bacon rashers
2 Add 175g (6oz) diced cooked ox tongue to the puréed mixture

Smoked Salmon Pâté

Serves 10-12
1-2 garlic cloves
550g (1¼lb) smoked salmon
100g (40z) butter
freshly ground black pepper
cream
lemon juice

Variations
1 Combine all ingredients in a liquidiser or food processor. Melt the butter for a liquidiser; this is not necessary with a food processor
2 Taramasalata: Use smoked cod's roe in place of smoked salmon
3 Use smoked trout, mackerel or lightly cooked kippers in place of smoked salmon
4 Fresh Fish Pâté: Use cooked cod's roe or cooked white fish; flavour with anchovy essence and a little tomato purée. Make only a day before the party

Liver Pâté

Peel the garlic. Put the liver, pork or bacon, thyme and garlic once or twice through a mincer, depending on the smoothness desired, or into a liquidiser or food processor. Heat the butter, stir in the flour and cook for 2-3 minutes, then gradually blend in the milk. Bring to the boil, stirring until a thick sauce (a panada). Add the sauce and all the other ingredients to the minced meats, blending well. This stage can be carried out in a food processor. Butter a 0.75-lkg (1½-2lb) loaf tin, put in the mixture. Cover with well-buttered greaseproof paper or foil, or see Variation 1. Stand the tin in a bain-marie (a tin of water) and bake for 1¾ hours in the centre of a very moderate oven, 160°C, 325°F, Gas Mark 3. Place a light weight on top of the pâté as it cools.
    Serve with hot toast and butter, lettuce and lemon.

To freeze ahead
This freezes well for 1 month.

Smoked Salmon Pâté

Peel and crush the garlic (unless using a liquidiser or food processor, when the whole clove(s) can be added to the fish). Cut the salmon into small pieces, if using a liquidiser or food processor, or mince finely. Cream the butter, add the fish, garlic, and blend thoroughly, then add pepper to taste and gradually blend in sufficient cream to give the desired consistency; you will need approximately 150ml (¼pt). Use *unwhipped* double cream for a rich pâté, single cream for a lighter texture. Finally, add lemon juice to flavour. Spoon into a container and cover thoroughly. This can be made 2 or 3 days before the party. Serve with hot toast, butter and wedges of lemon.

To freeze ahead
This freezes well for up to 6 weeks. Allow to defrost at room temperature which takes several hours, or overnight in the refrigerator.

Soups

This is the course where you can produce something rather original; for example, few people in this country make fish soups, and whilst some are exotic and difficult, the recipe given on page 73 is easy to make and would appeal to the majority of people. This is a fairly sustaining soup and ideal, therefore, to precede a light main course.

Convenience soups are good, and brief hints for adding flavour are on the right. Nothing can compare with the flavour of freshly-made seasonal vegetable soups. The pea soup on page 71 (Potage St Germain), plus the other suggestions, will enable you to produce vegetable soups throughout the year.

Introduce soups from other countries, the Bortsch being a classic example of this. If they have the ability to be served hot or cold you can be 'in tune' with the weather. Do not disregard the appeal of cold soups; we are becoming more used to these in this country and they are ideal for the busy hostess.

Bortsch

Wash the beetroot very thoroughly, then peel and cut into very neat shreds or use a coarse grater. Peel the carrot and onion and cut these and the celery in a similar manner. It is important that the vegetables look an attractive shape, for this soup is not sieved. If serving the soup hot, the butter should be used unless the stock has a reasonable amount of fat. If serving the soup cold, omit the butter and use a stock without fat, as this will spoil the appearance of the soup when served. Heat the butter in a pan and toss the carrot, onion and celery in this, then add the stock or water and stock cubes, or simply put the vegetables into the liquid. Skin the tomatoes, cut into neat small slices. Add these to the soup with salt and pepper, bay leaves, vinegar or lemon juice and sugar if wished. Cover the pan and simmer gently for 1½ hours or until the beetroot is very tender. Remove the bay leaves. To prepare the garnish, peel and shred the beetroot, then stir into the soup with the dill or parsley, heat for a few minutes. Serve topped with the soured cream or yoghurt.

To keep the soup hot
Pour the soup into the heated dish of a Hostess trolley or cabinet or turn heat very low under the saucepan. Do not add the final garnish to the hot or cold soup until ready to serve.

To serve the soup cold
Chill well, add the garnish when serving.

To freeze ahead
This soup freezes well for 3 months.

Add flavour to

Canned Turtle Soup
Blend a little single or double cream and pinch of curry powder with hot or cold turtle soup. Serve as Lady Curzon soup.

Canned Consommé
Heat with a little sherry. Serve cold, topped with lemon wedges and lightly whipped, or soured, cream.

Canned Lobster Bisque
Heat in a double saucepan, add the yolks of 1-2 eggs blended with a little single cream, and 2-3tbspn white wine or dry sherry.

Bortsch

Serves 6
1 large raw beetroot
1 large carrot
1 large onion
1 stick of celery
25-50g (1-2oz) butter (optional
 — see method)
1.2L (2pt) beef stock or water
 and 2 beef stock cubes
3 medium tomatoes
salt and pepper
2 bay leaves
1tbspn vinegar or lemon juice
1 tspn sugar (optional)

To garnish
1 small cooked beetroot
1tbspn chopped dill or parsley
150ml (¼pt) soured cream or
 yoghurt

Gazpacho

Serves 8
water (see method)
1kg (2lb) ripe tomatoes
1 large cucumber
2 medium onions
2-3 garlic cloves
1 large green pepper
2-4tbspn olive oil
3-4tbspn white wine vinegar or
 lemon juice
salt and pepper
3-4 slices bread

Variation
Iced Tomato and Cucumber
Soup: Use the amount of
tomatoes, cucumber, onion and
garlic in the recipe above, but
omit the other ingredients.
Simmer with a little water until
a purée. Sieve or liquidise,
season well, flavour with
chopped parsley and chives.
Pour into freezing tray and
freeze very lightly, then spoon
into chilled soup cups. Top
with yoghurt or soured cream.

Vichyssoise

Serves 8-10
1kg (2lb) leeks
350g (12oz) old potatoes
 (weight when peeled)
75g (3oz) butter
1.5L (2½pt) chicken stock
salt and pepper
300ml (½pt) single or double
 cream
2tbspn chopped parsley
2-3tbspn chopped chives

Variations
Add a little white wine or flaked
crabmeat to the soup

Gazpacho

Chill the water in the refrigerator; this speeds the chilling of the
prepared soup. Skin the tomatoes, unless sieving the mixture; cut into
pieces. Peel and chop a generous half of the cucumber, 1 onion, the
garlic and half the pepper (discard the core and seeds); save the
remaining cucumber, onion and pepper for an accompaniment to the
soup. Add the chopped vegetables to the tomatoes and either sieve or
liquidise the mixture or pound until absolutely smooth. Tip into a
basin, add the olive oil (the amount used depends upon personal taste,
use the smaller amount if people are calorie-conscious), then the
vinegar or lemon juice and enough of the very cold water to make a
flowing consistency. Add salt and pepper to taste. Chill the soup very
thoroughly. Dice the rest of the cucumber, onion and pepper,
together with the bread, and put into individual dishes. Each guest
helps himself to the accompaniment.

   If serving for a buffet it may be easier to put the accompaniments on
top of the individual filled soup cups or tureen of soup.

To keep the food cold
Put the soup into a chilled soup tureen and chill the soup cups too, if
there is room in the refrigerator.

To freeze ahead
The basic puréed soup can be frozen for several months, but the
accompaniments must be freshly prepared.

Vichyssoise

Cut the tough, darker green part away from the leeks and discard it,
but leave a little of the pale green as this helps to give an attractive
colour. Slice the leeks; peel and slice the potatoes. Heat the butter in a
saucepan and toss the leeks and potatoes in this; do not allow to colour.
Add the stock, with a little salt and pepper. Cover the pan and simmer
for about 20 minutes or until the vegetables are just tender. Do not
overcook as this spoils the colour of the soup. Sieve or liquidise the
mixture, cool; add the cream and half the parsley and chives. Chill
well. Top with the remaining herbs.

To keep the food cold
See the comments under Gazpacho above.

To freeze ahead
The vegetable purée freezes moderately well for up to 3 months. It
may separate during freezing, so sieve or liquidise again.

Stocks and Consommé

Good stock is often the essence of an outstanding soup. The pea soup below depends upon the delicate flavour of a ham stock. You obtain this from simmering boiling bacon in water; you could use chicken stock instead and add bacon rinds to the ingredients.

Simmer meat, poultry or game bones for meat stocks and the bones and skin of fish for fish stock. Vegetables could be added.

A consommé is, however, quite different, for you need a more concentrated flavour for this classic soup. First prepare a beef stock, strain this carefully. Return to the saucepan, add a good 450g (1lb) diced shin of beef to each 2L (3½pt) stock. Season well, then simmer for at least 2 hours or allow 30-45 minutes at H/15lb in a pressure cooker. Strain the meat-flavoured liquid through fine muslin; serve as described on the right.

Creamed Vegetable Soups

Use the recipe for Potage St Germain, below, as the basis for vegetable soups. Prepare asparagus, cauliflower, Jerusalem artichokes or leeks instead of peas. Chicken stock is better for these particular vegetables, so use this instead of ham stock. Top with croûtons.

Potage St Germain

Peel and slice the onions. Melt the butter or margarine in a pan and toss the onions in this, add the ham stock and peas, or peas and pods. Season well; this soup should have plenty of pepper so peppercorns as well as a shake of pepper can be put in. Add the mint. Cover the pan and simmer gently for 45 minutes. Strain the liquid, remove the peppercorns and mint, then sieve or liquidise the peas, pea pods and onion. Return to the liquid. Blend the milk with the flour, stir into the soup, bring slowly to the boil and cook until thickened. Add the cream just before serving. Garnish with croûtons and parsley.

To keep the food hot
The inclusion of cream means this soup must be kept hot with care. Pour into the heated dish of a Hostess trolley or cabinet or into a tureen, cover well and place this on to a heat tray or into a cool oven. You can pour the cooked soup into a basin or the top of a double saucepan and stand over hot, but not boiling, water; cover tightly.

To freeze ahead
This soup freezes well for 3 months. Cook as above, sieve or liquidise, then cool and freeze. Add the cream when reheating

Additions to Consommé

Remember cold or lightly iced consommé is excellent.
1 Flavour the consommé with dry or brown sherry.
2 Blend hot or cold consommé with tomato juice to make a speedy Madrilène soup. Top with skinned, diced tomatoes.
3 Top consommé with narrow strips of cooked pancakes, with diced cooked vegetables, with a little yoghurt or soured cream.
4 Top with fried croûtons. To make these cut bread into small dice. Deep-fry in oil or shallow-fry in butter until crisp and brown. Drain on absorbent paper. Keep hot as page 45.

Potage St Germain

Serves 6
1-2 medium onions
25g (1oz) butter or margarine
900ml (1½pt) ham stock
350g (12oz) shelled peas or 675g
   (1½lb) peas and pods
salt and pepper
6-8 peppercorns (optional)
small bunch of mint
150ml (¼pt) milk
15g (½oz) flour
4tbspn single or double cream

To garnish
croûtons
1-2tbspn chopped parsley

Note: If using peas and pods, shell the peas; save and wash about half the pods; choose just the young, green fleshy ones

71

Salmon Chowder

De-rind the bacon and cut it into matchstick shapes. Peel and grate the onion. Heat the butter in a pan and fry the bacon and onion for several minutes; do not allow the onion to discolour. Add the fish stock or water and stock cube and lemon juice. Bring to the boil. Peel and grate or dice the potato, dice fresh uncooked salmon and add to the liquid together with salt and pepper to taste; simmer for 10 minutes. If using canned salmon, flake this and add to the liquid when the potato is nearly cooked. Blend the flour with the milk, stir into the soup, bring slowly to the boil, cook until thickened. Add the cream, but do not cook further. Garnish with parsley or fennel.

To keep the food hot
The blending of cream and lemon juice means this soup must be kept hot with care. Pour into the heated dish of a Hostess trolley or cabinet or into a tureen and place this on to a heat tray or into a cool oven. You can pour the cooked soup into a basin or the top of a double saucepan and stand over hot, but not boiling, water.

To freeze ahead
This soup is better freshly made. It is an excellent way of using frozen salmon.

Turkey Tarragon Soup

Peel and chop the onion; break or cut the carcass into joints, place into a large saucepan. Add the giblets, onion, bay leaf, mace, peppercorns and a little salt and pepper, with enough cold water to just cover. Bring the liquid to the boil; cover the pan, lower the heat and simmer for 45 minutes to 1 hour (or pressure cook at H/15lb pressure for 15 minutes). Remove carcass, strain, but reserve the stock; pick the meat from the carcass and the giblets; chop neatly. Put the turkey carcass back into the liquid in a saucepan or open pressure cooker; do not cover. Reduce the stock by open-boiling until about 1L (1¾pt).

Blend the cornflour with a little of the cold milk, add to the stock, with the remaining milk. Finely chop the celery, put into the pan with the stock mixture. Bring to the boil, stirring all the time, until a smooth, slightly thickened liquid. Cover and cook gently for 10 minutes, or for 2 minutes at H/15lb pressure, to soften the celery. Remove the lid, add the chopped turkey meat, together with the tarragon, the cream and seasoning to taste. Heat for 1-2 minutes.

Sprinkle the fried croûtons on to the soup just before serving. See colour picture opposite.

To keep the food hot
As the Potage St Germain, page 71. The croûtons must be kept on a flat plate over absorbent paper until ready to serve.

To freeze ahead
As the Potage St Germain on page 71.

Salmon Chowder

Serves 6
2 rashers bacon
1 small onion
25g (1oz) butter
600ml (1pt) fish stock or water with ½ chicken stock cube
½tbspn lemon juice
1 large potato
225g (8oz) salmon (weight without skin and bones) or 227g (8oz) can of salmon
salt and pepper
25g (1oz) flour
300ml (½pt) milk
150ml (¼pt) single cream

To garnish
chopped parsley or fennel

Variation
Use shell or diced white fish instead of salmon

Turkey Tarragon Soup

Serves 8
1 large onion
1 turkey carcass
1 set of turkey giblets
1 bay leaf
1 blade mace
6 black peppercorns
salt and pepper
40g (1½oz) cornflour
300ml (½pt) milk
3 sticks celery
2tspn chopped fresh or ¾tspn dried tarragon
150ml (¼pt) single cream

To garnish
fried croûtons

Variation
This is an excellent basic poultry soup, which can be made with the carcass of a large chicken, plus just a little cooked chicken flesh

(opposite) Turkey Tarragon Soup

To prepare Lobster and Crab

Allow one medium or half a large lobster per person. Slit the body down the centre; remove the long thin intestinal vein; crack the large claws. Page 16 gives information on finger bowls and lobster picks.
Allow a small to medium crab per person. Follow the directions given under Devilled Crab (page 75) for opening the body of the fish. Keep the light and dark crabmeat apart, then flake the fish. Spoon the light meat into half the shell and the dark meat into the other half. Garnish with parsley and a line of chopped hard-boiled egg.

Moules à la Marinière

Serves 4 as a main course or 6 as an hors d'oeuvre

3L (5pt) mussels
1 medium onion
small bunch parsley
1 bay leaf
300ml (½pt) white wine, preferably dry
salt and pepper
40g (1½oz) butter

Variation
Add up to 150ml (¼pt) double cream to the mussels and wine when reheating

Fish Dishes

This section is relatively short, for fish is not an ideal dish for a hot course unless you have help in the kitchen. Fish could be served if you are omitting an hors d'oeuvre or soup for a light luncheon menu. Cold fish dishes cause no problems.

Fish Meunière

This method of cooking fish is one of the simplest and most delicious; the fish also keeps hot for a limited time without spoiling. It is suitable for fresh trout, halibut, turbot or sole. Prepare the fish, then coat in a very little flour, mixed with salt and pepper. To 6 portions of fish allow 150g (good 5oz) butter. Heat this in a pan, cook the fish until just tender, put on to a hot dish. Add 2tbspn lemon juice, 2tbspn chopped parsley and 2tspn capers to the butter in the pan, heat until golden, spoon over the fish.

Lobster and Crab

These shellfish make delicious party dishes. The fishmonger will prepare (dress) crab, but see the lefthand column and page 75. Serve the lobster or crab in their shells, or on lettuce, with mayonnaise (recipe page 64), mixed salads and new potatoes.

Moules à la Marinière

Discard any mussels which are cracked or slightly open, then wash and scrub well; scrape away the beard (weed-like growth). Wash several times in cold water. Peel and finely chop the onion. Put the mussels into a large saucepan with the onion, a sprig of parsley, the bay leaf, wine, salt and pepper. Cover the pan and shake over a brisk heat for approximately 5 minutes or until all the shells have opened. Pull away the top shells; discard any fish that have not opened, return the mussels on the half shells to the liquid with the butter. You can keep the fish and liquid in the refrigerator until just before the meal, then remove the sprig of parsley. Chop and add several tablespoons of parsley to the liquid and fish. Heat for about 4 minutes, then serve in individual bowls. The mussels are eaten with the fingers and the liquid with a spoon. See colour picture on page 11.

To keep the food hot
These are better served as soon as reheated.

To freeze ahead
The fish is better served freshly cooked.

Trout with Dijon Sauce

Remove the heads and backbones from the trout. Peel and chop the onions finely, blend two-thirds with 2tbspn each of the parsley, tarragon, chives and all the watercress. Cream half the butter, add the onion and herb mixture, salt and pepper. Divide into 8 portions; spread over the inside of the trout. Fold the fish so they look whole again. Put into an oven-proof dish, add the wine or cider. Cover and bake in the centre of a moderate oven, 190°C, 375°F, Gas Mark 5, for 20 minutes or until just tender. Meanwhile heat the remaining butter in a saucepan, add the rest of the onions, cook gently for several minutes; stir in the flour, then the milk. Bring to the boil, stir until a smooth sauce. Lift the trout on to a heated serving dish. Strain the wine or cider into the hot, but not boiling, sauce. Add the remaining herbs, salt and pepper to taste, the mustard and, lastly, the cream. Heat the sauce gently; do not allow to boil, otherwise it could curdle. Slice the lemons and pepper. Spoon a little sauce over each trout, top with lemon and red pepper. Serve the remaining sauce in a heated sauceboat. See colour picture on page 97.

To keep the food hot
See 'Fish' and 'Sauces' on page 42.

To freeze ahead
The trout can be prepared and frozen for up to 3 months. Cook without defrosting.

Devilled Crab

Remove all the flesh from the body of the crabs and the meat from the large claws; save the tiny claws to garnish the dish. Discard the stomach bag and the grey fingers. Clean the shells with soft paper and polish with a little oil as these are used for serving the crabmeat. Flake the crabmeat, mixing light and dark meat together. Blend with 25g (1oz) of the breadcrumbs. Meanwhile heat the butter in a pan and fry the remaining breadcrumbs until well coated, but do not allow to brown. Flavour the crabmeat mixture with the salt, pepper, curry powder and sauce. Spoon into the shells and top with the buttered crumbs. Brown under a moderately hot grill or towards the top of a hot oven, 220°C, 425°F, Gas Mark 7. Lift on to a serving dish and garnish with the small crab claws, parsley and lemon.

To keep the food hot
Do not cover the filled crab shells. Keep in the hot cupboard of the Hostess or on a heat tray. You must have an oven at a very low temperature, otherwise the crab mixture dries; garnish the dish just before serving.

To freeze ahead
Prepare, but do not cook, the dish; freeze and use within 1 month. Cook as soon as defrosted; crab, like all shellfish, is highly perishable.

Trout with Dijon Sauce

Serves 8
8 medium fresh trout

For the stuffing and sauce
3 small onions
3tbspn chopped parsley
3tbspn chopped tarragon
3tbspn chopped chives
4tbspn chopped watercress
　leaves
100g (4oz) butter
salt and pepper
150ml (¼pt) dry white wine or
　cider
50g (2oz) flour
600ml (1pt) milk
3tspn Dijon mustard
150ml (¼pt) double cream

To garnish
2 lemons
1 canned red pepper

Variation
Use 2-3tspn made English mustard for a hotter-flavoured sauce

Devilled Crab

Serves 4
4 small crabs
little oil
75g (3oz) soft breadcrumbs
50g (2oz) butter
salt
good shake cayenne pepper
½-1tspn curry powder
1tspn Worcestershire sauce

To garnish
chopped parsley
lemon wedges

Variation
For a hotter flavour add a few drops of Tabasco sauce, and 1-2tspn made mustard; mix very well

Plaice Gougère (see opposite)

Salmon Walewska

Put the salmon into an oven-proof dish. Melt 25g (1oz) butter; leave the remainder at room temperature to soften. Brush the salmon with the melted butter. Sprinkle with ½tbspn lemon juice and add a little salt and pepper. Cover the dish with foil; bake for 20-25 minutes in the centre of a moderate oven, 180-190°C, 350-375°F, Gas Mark 4-5, until just tender — do NOT over-cook. Lift on to a serving dish.

Meanwhile make the sauce. Put the egg yolks, a little salt and pepper and the remaining lemon juice into a basin; stand over a pan of hot, but not boiling, water and whisk until thick. Gradually whisk in the rest of the butter then add the diced pieces of lobster. Top the salmon with the sauce and garnish with the lemon and cucumber. If using fresh lobster use some of the small claws for garnish.

To keep the food hot
This is such a delicate dish that it should be served as soon as possible after cooking. If you need to keep it hot, see under 'Fish' on page 42.

To freeze ahead
Do not freeze the completed dish, but frozen salmon could be used.

Plaice Gougère

Roll up the fish fillets (securing with cocktail sticks), place in an oven-proof dish. Dot with butter and salt and pepper and bake for 20 minutes in the centre of a moderate oven, 180°C, 350°F, Gas Mark 4. Grate all the cheese. Melt 25g (1oz) butter or margarine, stir in the flour. Cook for 1 minute over a gentle heat without browning. Gradually add the liquid, stir well after each addition. Bring to the boil, stirring all the time. Simmer for 2-3 minutes. Add 75g (3oz) of the grated cheese.

Prepare the choux pastry as page 109, then add the remaining cheese to this. Grease an oven-proof serving dish. Spoon or pipe the pastry into this to form a border, leave a hollow in the centre. Lift the plaice fillets into the centre, spoon the cheese sauce over them, being careful not to cover the pastry. These preparations could be made an hour or two ahead. Bake in the centre of a moderately hot oven, 200°C, 400°F, Gas Mark 6, for approximately 30 minutes or until the pastry is golden and firm. See colour picture opposite.

To keep the food hot
Serve as soon as cooked; do not freeze the cooked dish.

A Gougère, prepared and baked from choux pastry as above, is an excellent way to serve cooked foods. It can be served hot or cold. Fill with poultry, meat, fish and vegetables in an appropriate sauce.

Salmon Walewska

Serves 4
4 cutlets salmon

For the Hollandaise sauce
100g (4oz) butter
1½tbspn lemon juice
salt and pepper
3 egg yolks
approximately 100g (4oz)
    lobster meat

To garnish
lemon slices
cucumber slices

Note: This is one way of cooking salmon cutlets; you can also wrap each cutlet in oiled greaseproof paper (if serving cold) or buttered paper (if serving hot). Put the fish into a pan of boiling salted water, then simmer for 10 minutes per 450g (1lb).

Plaice Gougère

Serves 4-6
4-6 plaice fillets
40g (1½oz) butter
salt and pepper

For the cheese sauce
75g (3oz) Gruyère or Cheddar
    cheese
25g (1oz) butter or margarine
25g (1oz) flour
300ml (½pt) milk

choux pastry (page 109) plus
    50g (2oz) Gruyère or
    Cheddar cheese

Variations
Use portions of halibut, turbot or fresh salmon instead of plaice

Stuffings

Choice of Stuffings

For Fish

Parsley and Thyme stuffing is ideal; this can be adapted as suggested under the recipe. You also could add 1-2 skinned and chopped tomatoes or 50g (2oz) sliced raw mushrooms.

For Chicken, Turkey and Veal

Although Sage and Onion stuffing is often used, the more traditional Parsley and Thyme and/or Chestnut stuffing are more appropriate.
The Forcemeat Balls add a pleasing contrast in texture.

For Duck, Goose and Pork

Use Sage and Onion stuffing. You could add 2 peeled and diced dessert apples.

For Lamb or Beef

Beef is rarely stuffed, but if you follow the suggestion on page 90 the Forcemeat Balls mixture is ideal; make this slightly less stiff. Any of the stuffings given on this page are acceptable for lamb, but a fruit-flavoured mixture makes a change. Prepare the ingredients as Parsley and Thyme stuffing but omit the egg. Add up to 225g (8oz) drained and chopped canned apricots or pineapple. Mix the stuffing with fruit syrup instead of the egg.

To Cook Stuffings

Stuffings are generally put inside, or with, the fish, meat or poultry, but it may be advisable to cook these separately for easy serving, or if you are unsure if your guests like the flavour. Put the mixture into a dish, cover tightly. Cook for 30-45 minutes, depending upon the oven temperature.

A well-flavoured stuffing adds interest to many fish, meat and poultry dishes. The ingredients give 6-8 good portions.

Chestnut
Split the skins of 450g (1lb) chestnuts, boil in water to cover for 10 minutes, no longer, otherwise they break as you remove the skins. Drain, skin while warm. Put the nuts into 450ml (¾pt) ham stock, simmer gently until tender; strain, but keep a little stock. Sieve or liquidise the nuts until a purée. Add 225g (8oz) chopped cooked ham or bacon, 50g (2oz) soft breadcrumbs and 50g (2oz) butter, bind with stock.

Canned chestnut purée can be used instead of fresh chestnuts; in this case, add a few chopped hazelnuts or walnuts for texture.

Parsley and Thyme
Shred 100g (4oz) suet, or melt the same amount of butter or margarine; blend with 225g (8oz) soft breadcrumbs, 3tbspn chopped parsley, the grated rind and juice of 1 lemon, 1tspn chopped fresh, or ½tspn dried thyme, 2 eggs and salt and pepper to taste.

This basic stuffing can be varied, eg add a little finely chopped bacon, or the finely-chopped cooked giblet meat from poultry.

A rice stuffing is made by substituting 225g (8oz) cooked rice for the breadcrumbs. Use either round or long grain rice.

Sage and Onion
Peel 3 large onions, put into a saucepan with 450ml (¾pt) water. Simmer steadily for about 20 minutes when the onions will be partly cooked. Remove the onions on to a chopping board, chop into small pieces. Shred 50-75g (2-3oz) suet or melt the same amount of butter or margarine. Mix with the onions, 75g (3oz) soft breadcrumbs, 3tspn chopped fresh, or 1½ tspn dried sage, 1 egg (optional), salt and pepper to taste. Add a little onion stock, if wished, to give a more moist mixture. You will need this if not using the egg. The stuffing tends to be less solid if the egg is omitted.

You can chop the raw onions and blend with the other ingredients; this gives a more definite flavour to the stuffing.

Forcemeat Balls
Finely chop or mince 3 rashers of bacon, blend with 175g (6oz) soft breadcrumbs, 75g (3oz) shredded suet or the same quantity of melted butter or margarine, 1½-2tbspn chopped parsley, 1½tspn chopped fresh, or ¾tspn dried mixed herbs, the grated rind of 1 lemon, 1 egg, and salt and pepper to taste. Form the mixture into balls about the size of a large walnut and put into a well-greased and pre-heated tin. Cook for 30-45 minutes.

The term 'Forcemeat Balls' can be applied to balls made from the Parsley and Thyme stuffing, recipe above, or balls based on sausagemeat. To make these, blend 450g (1lb) sausagemeat, 75g (3oz) soft white or brown breadcrumbs, 2-3tbspn chopped parsley, or use a mixture of herbs, such as parsley, chives and sage, and bind with an egg. Cook as the basic recipe above.

Sauces

There are a number of special sauces throughout this book, but the following are classic sauces. The amounts given serve 6-8.

Apple
Peel and slice 675g (1½lb) cooking apples. Put into a saucepan with 3 tbspn water and 50g (2oz) sugar. Cook until tender. Add 50g (2oz) butter towards the end of the cooking period. Beat briskly, sieve or liquidise to give a smooth purée.

Bread
Peel a small onion, press 3-4 cloves into this if you are sure everyone likes these. Put the onion and 450ml (¾pt) milk into a saucepan. Bring the milk to the boil, remove from the heat and add 75g (3oz) breadcrumbs, salt and pepper and 50g (2oz) butter. Cover and leave in a warm place to infuse. Reheat just before the meal. Remove the onion; stir briskly before serving. It is wiser to cook Bread Sauce in the top of a double saucepan or basin over hot water, so there is no fear or it burning. 2-3 tbspn double cream can be added.

Cranberry
Put 5tbspn water and 110g (4oz) sugar into a saucepan; stir until the sugar has dissolved. Add 450g (1lb) cranberries, 4tbspn redcurrant jelly and simmer in a covered pan until the cranberries are soft. 2tbspn port wine could be added in place of this amount of water.

Mint
Chop enough mint leaves to give 8tbspn. Blend with 50-75g (2-3oz) sugar and 6tbspn white or brown malt vinegar.

Orange
Cut away the peel from 3 large sweet oranges, remove the white pith and cut the orange-coloured 'zest' into matchstick pieces. Put into 200ml (7½ fl oz) water, soak for 30 minutes, then simmer gently for about 15 minutes or until tender. Blend 450ml (¾pt) duck or goose stock with 3tspn arrowroot or cornflour and strain into the saucepan containing the orange mixture. Add 3tbspn redcurrant jelly, 2tspn lemon juice, salt, pepper and 3tspn sugar. Stir well as you bring the mixture to the boil, then continue to cook until thickened

Hollandaise Sauce

Put 50-100g (2-4oz) butter on one side to soften. Place 3 egg yolks, 1-1½tbspn lemon juice or white wine vinegar, salt and pepper to taste, in the top of a double saucepan or basin. Stand over a pan of hot, but not boiling, water on a low heat, whip until thick and creamy; gradually whisk in the butter. If using a liquidiser or food processor, whisk the egg yolks etc in that, add the very hot melted butter steadily.

Savoury Mousseline Sauce is made as above, using the smaller amount of butter, then adding 3-4tbspn double cream.

White Sauce
Heat 25g (1oz) butter or margarine in a saucepan, add 25g (1oz) flour, stir over a low heat for 2-3 minutes, then gradually blend in 300ml (½pt) milk. Bring to the boil, stirring well, add salt and pepper to taste. Lower the heat, cook gently until the sauce coats the back of a wooden spoon. See page 42 for keeping sauces hot.

Variations
Add these after the sauce has thickened:
1 Anchovy: Flavour the sauce with 2-3 chopped anchovy fillets or a few drops of anchovy essence
2 Cheese: Add 50-100g (2-4oz) grated Cheddar, Gouda, Gruyère, or other cheese
3 Horseradish: Add 1-2tbspn grated fresh horseradish
4 Parsley: Blend in 2tbspn finely chopped parsley

Choice of Sauces

For Fish and Vegetables
White Sauce or a variation given below, Hollandaise or Mousseline Sauce.

For Chicken, Turkey or Veal
Bread Sauce or Cranberry Sauce are equally good, or serve both, as they complement each other.

For Duck, Goose or Pork
The rich flesh needs the bite of fruit, such as an Apple or Orange Sauce.

For Lamb and Beef
Choose Mint Sauce for the former or Horseradish Sauce or Cream (page 63) for beef.

(overleaf left) Colonial Goose (see page 90)

(overleaf right) Bacon with Marinade Sauce and Duchesse Potatoes, and Chocolate Mousse (see page 52)

Accompaniments to Game

Bacon Rolls

Cut the rind from streaky rashers. Stretch with the back of a knife, halve and roll. Secure with metal skewers and cook in the oven for 15-20 minutes.

Game (potato) Crisps

Peel and cut potatoes into wafer-thin slices. Deep fry in hot oil for 2-3 minutes, drain on absorbent paper. To keep hot and crisp, spread out on a flat dish; place in the hot cupboard of the Hostess or in a very cool oven.

Fried Crumbs

Make rather coarse breadcrumbs from a white loaf. Deep fry in oil or shallow fry in butter. Keep hot as Game Crisps.

Yorkshire Pudding

Serves 8-10
225g (8oz) flour, preferably plain
pinch salt
2 eggs
575ml (1pt) milk, or milk and water (do not use 600ml)

For greasing tin(s)
25-40g (1-1½oz) fat

Piquant Sauce

Serves 8
1 large onion
2tbspn meat dripping
25g (1oz) flour
300ml (½pt) red wine
1tbspn Worcestershire sauce
juices from cooking meat (see method)
2tbspn redcurrant jelly

Meat, Poultry and Game

A great diversity of dishes based upon these foods can be selected when entertaining. A modern way of presenting meat is to wrap it in pastry, ie to serve it 'en croûte'. This is practical, as well as being delicious, for the dish can be prepared in advance; the pastry helps to keep the meat moist, and the final result is very impressive. Recipes are on page 84. A meat pie has similar advantages, and a recipe which could be adapted by using different meats, instead of steak and pheasant, is on page 83.

Roasting will always be a popular method of cooking especially when entertaining a large group of people. This subject is dealt with on pages 89-94 and there are numerous suggestions for adding a 'new look' to a traditional roast.

The usual accompaniments to roast game are given on the left, and a Yorkshire Pudding, which to many people is an essential partner to roast beef, below. This is followed by a flavoursome sauce to serve with various meats, or as an excellent basis for a Salmis (see page 87).

Yorkshire Pudding

Use Temperature 1 as page 92.
Blend all the ingredients except the fat together to give a smooth batter. Small puddings are easier to serve, so thickly grease 16-20 deep patty tins with the fat. Pre-heat in the hot oven for 4-5 minutes, spoon in the batter. Bake for 12-15 minutes towards the top of the oven until well-risen and firm. If you decide to bake a large pudding, cook for 35-40 minutes, reducing the heat slightly after 20 minutes.

Lift the pudding(s) from the tin(s) on to a hot dish, stand in the Hostess hot cupboard, on a heat tray or in a cool oven. See colour picture on page 93.

Piquant Sauce

Peel and finely chop the onion. Heat the reserved dripping from the meat in a saucepan, add the onion and fry gently for 5 minutes. Stir in the flour and cook for 2-3 minutes. Gradually stir in the wine, Worcestershire sauce and any reserved meat juices from roasting the meat. Bring to the boil, stirring all the time. Add the redcurrant jelly, cover the pan and simmer gently for 10 minutes.

This sauce has a pleasant mixture of a savoury and sweet flavour. It is a good sauce upon which to base a Salmis (see page 87).

Steak and Pheasant Pie

Meat pies are a general favourite, and a really interesting filling topped with light-as-a-feather pastry is a dish 'par excellence'.

Make the pastry, for it needs time to stand. Sieve the flour and salt into a mixing bowl. Add the lemon juice and enough water to make an elastic dough; roll out to an oblong shape. Place the butter in the centre of the pastry dough. Bring up the bottom third of the dough, bring down the top third, so completely covering the butter. Turn the pastry at right angles, seal the open ends, depress at intervals with the rolling pin, giving a ribbed effect; roll out again. Repeat the folding, turning and rolling action to give 7 rollings and 7 foldings. The pastry must be allowed to rest in the refrigerator between each of these, and before using.

To make the filling, cut the steak, pheasants and pheasant livers into neat pieces. Remove the bones. Put the bones into a saucepan with water to cover and a little salt and pepper. Cover the pan and simmer for an hour. Strain the liquid and measure out 450ml (¾pt). Peel and dice the onions, wipe, but do not peel the mushrooms. Blend the flour, salt and pepper, then coat the beef and pheasant. Heat the butter in a large saucepan; fry the meat and game for 8-10 minutes and add the onions and mushrooms after 5 minutes, stirring well to prevent the mixture burning. Gradually blend in the pheasant stock and wine; stir over a low heat until the sauce comes to the boil and thickens slightly. Spoon the beef, pheasant and vegetables into a 2.5L (4½pt) pie dish, with just enough sauce to cover, then allow to cool. Save the remaining sauce to serve separately.

Roll out the pastry thinly, cut a long strip; press this around the rim of the pie dish. Cover the filling with the puff pastry. Trim away the surplus pastry, flute and flake the edges of the pie. Make a slit on top for the steam to escape. Use any pastry left over to make a 'tassel' and 'leaves'. Beat the egg, and brush over the pastry. Bake the pie in the centre of a hot oven, 220°C, 425°F, Gas Mark 7 for 25-30 minutes until the pastry is well-risen and golden; lower the heat to moderate, 180°C, 350°F, Gas Mark 4 for a further 30 minutes.

To keep the food hot
Place the pie in the hot cupboard of a Hostess trolley or cabinet, on a heat tray, or in a cool oven. Do not cover the pastry.

To freeze ahead
This pie freezes well for 3 months.

Steak and Pheasant Pie

Serves 8-10
For the puff pastry
225g (8oz) plain flour
pinch salt
½tbspn lemon juice
ice-cold water
225g (8oz) butter

For the filling
450g (1lb) rump steak
2 large pheasants with giblets
salt and pepper
2 large onions
175g (6oz) small button
  mushrooms
40g (1½oz) flour
50g (2oz) butter
pheasant stock (see method)
150ml (¼pt) red wine

To glaze
1 egg

Variations
1 Chicken and Ham Pie: Use ham in place of beef; a large chicken instead of pheasants, and white wine or extra stock or double cream in place of red wine
2 For a quicker topping buy 450g (1lb) frozen puff pastry. This amount, or the pastry produced by the amounts in the recipe above, must be rolled thinly to cover a big pie dish. Remember puff pastry rises to about 5 times the original thickness
3 Steak and Pheasant Picnic Pie: Make short crust pastry with 600g (1lb 4oz) flour and 300g (10oz) fat (see page 109). Roll out, use half to line a 25-28cm (10-11in) flan dish or tin. Fill with the steak and pheasant mixture, but 2-3tbspn sauce only. Top with pastry, bake as method on the right

Gala Topside of Beef

Serves 8
1 small onion
100g (4oz) mushrooms
1.35kg (3lb) joint of topside of
     beef
salt and pepper
25g (1oz) butter
113g (4oz) can liver pâté
1 tbspn Worcestershire sauce
puff pastry made with 175g
     (6oz) flour, etc (page 83) OR
     370g (13oz) frozen puff
     pastry
1 egg

To garnish
parsley

To serve
Piquant Sauce (page 82)

Variations
1 Use a joint of cooked ham or
bacon instead of beef; do not
salt the meat
2 Lightly cooked lamb cutlets
can be coated with the pâté
mixture and pastry. Bake for 30
minutes

Lamb en Croûte

Serves 8
1 boned leg of lamb
½-1tspn chopped fresh or
     ¼tspn dried rosemary and
     sage
salt and pepper
puff pastry made as the recipe
     above
1 egg

Gala Topside of Beef

Peel and finely chop the onion; wipe then chop the mushrooms. Season the beef with salt and pepper, wrap loosely in foil, place in a roasting tin and roast in the centre of a moderate oven (Temperature 2, page 92) until cooked. Remove from the oven, allow to cool. Take the joint out of the foil, reserve all the dripping and meat juices from the tin.

Heat the butter in a saucepan, add the onion, fry gently for 5 minutes. Add the mushrooms and cook for a further minute. Blend with the pâté and Worcestershire sauce, mix well and leave to cool. Roll out the pastry to a rectangle large enough to enclose the joint. Trim the pastry edges. Spread the pâté mixture over the pastry, leaving a 5cm (2in) border. Place the joint in the centre of the pastry. Beat the egg, brush the edges of the pastry with this and bring them together to enclose the beef completely. Seal the edges well. Place the pastry-wrapped joint on a piece of greased foil in the roasting tin with the pastry seams underneath. Roll out the pastry trimmings, cut out leaves for decoration, brush with egg and arrange on top of the pastry. Brush beaten egg all over the pastry and bake in the centre of a hot oven, 220°C, 425°F, Gas Mark 7, for 30-40 minutes, until the pastry is golden brown. Look in the oven after 20-25 minutes and reduce the heat slightly if the pastry is cooking too quickly. Prepare the Piquant Sauce (page 82) while the pastry cooks. Garnish the joint with the parsley and serve with the sauce.

To keep the food hot
Lift on to a heated dish, garnish with the parsley and place in the hot cupboard of a Hostess trolley or cabinet, in a cool oven or on a heat tray. Do not cover.

To freeze ahead
The best way to freeze 'en croûte' dishes is to cook the meat, allow to cool, wrap in pastry as the recipe, but do not cook the dish. Open-freeze then wrap. Defrost thoroughly then continue cooking as above. Use within 3 months.

Lamb en Croûte

Weigh the meat, sprinkle with the herbs, salt and pepper, then tie into a neat shape. Roast at Temperature 2 (page 92) but be careful not to over-cook the meat. Allow to cool. Roll out the pastry very thinly until sufficiently large to cover the leg. Place the meat in the centre of the pastry. Beat the egg, brush the edges of the pastry with this and bring them together to enclose the meat. Seal the edges, then continue as the recipe for Gala Topside of Beef above. See colour picture opposite.

(opposite) Lamb en Croûte

Chicken Basquaise

Serves 6
1 garlic clove
1 medium onion
1 green pepper
2-3 canned red peppers
50g (2oz) butter
2tbspn oil
6 chicken portions
25g (1oz) flour
300ml (½pt) chicken stock or
    water and ½ chicken stock
    cube
150ml (¼pt) white wine
2tspn tomato purée
1tspn paprika
salt and pepper
chopped parsley

To garnish
sprig of parsley

Turkey Stroganoff

Serves 8
900g (2lb) turkey breast meat
salt and black pepper
100g (4oz) butter
2tbspn oil
2 medium onions
2 garlic cloves
225g (8oz) mushrooms
300ml (½pt-10 fl oz) soured
    cream
4tbspn apple juice

To garnish
chopped parsley

To serve
450g (1lb) cooked brown rice

Variations
1 Use brandy in place of apple
juice
2 Beef Stroganoff: Use strips of
tender fillet steak in place of
turkey

Chicken Basquaise

Peel and crush the garlic, slice the onion; cut the peppers into thin slices, discard the core and seeds from the green pepper. Heat the butter and oil in a large frying pan. Fry the chicken with the garlic until golden brown, remove from the pan and put into a casserole. Fry the onion and peppers until soft, then add the flour to the fat remaining in the pan, stir well and cook over a low heat for 2-3 minutes. Add the stock, or water and stock cube, wine, tomato purée, paprika, together with salt and pepper to taste. Stir for several minutes, add the chopped parsley. Pour the sauce over the chicken, cover the casserole and cook in the centre of a moderate oven, 180°C, 350°F, Gas Mark 4, for 40-45 minutes. Top with parsley and serve with cooked rice. See colour picture on page 19.

To keep the food hot
As page 87. Keep well covered.

To freeze ahead
This freezes well; use within 3 months.

Turkey Stroganoff

Cut away the breast from a large turkey or buy turkey breast joints. Cut the meat into strips measuring approximately 7.5 x 1cm (3 x ½in). Sprinkle these with salt and pepper. Heat the butter and oil in a large frying pan and gently fry the turkey meat until cooked and tender. This takes about 12-15 minutes; move the turkey as it fries, so that it is evenly cooked. Meanwhile peel and slice the onions, peel and chop the garlic, wipe then slice the mushrooms. Remove the turkey from the pan and keep warm. Fry the onion, garlic and mushrooms in the remaining fat until lightly browned. Strain off surplus fat. Add the soured cream and apple juice, heat gently but do not allow to boil. Return the turkey meat to the pan. Transfer to a warmed serving dish; garnish with chopped parsley. Serve with the brown rice, cooked as directed on page 114. See colour picture on page 15.

To keep the food hot
A Hostess serving dish can be used, or cover the food on a flat serving dish, so the turkey mixture does not dry. Keep hot in the cupboard of a Hostess trolley or cabinet, or on a heat tray or in a cool oven.

To freeze ahead
Cook all the ingredients very lightly so they are not overcooked when reheated. Use within 3 months. Reheat in the oven or in a little extra heated butter in a frying pan.

Turkey à la King

Slice the mushrooms and pepper, discard the core and seeds. Heat the butter in a frying pan, add the mushrooms and pepper, cook gently until soft. Heat the butter for the sauce in a large saucepan, stir in the flour, then gradually blend in the milk and stock, add salt and pepper to taste. Bring to the boil, cook until thickened, stirring well; remove from the heat. Blend the eggs and cream together, then whisk into the hot, but not boiling, sauce. Cook gently without boiling for 2-3 minutes. Cut the turkey into neat pieces, add to the sauce with the cooked mushrooms and pepper and heat together for a few minutes. Put into a heated serving dish. Cover tightly. Cut the bread in neat triangles. Heat the butter in a frying pan. Fry the bread until crisp and brown. Top the turkey mixture with the parsley; add the fried bread *immediately* before serving. See colour picture on page 53.

To keep the food hot
Keep the turkey mixture tightly covered. A Hostess dish is ideal, or a covered casserole on a heat tray. The fried bread should be kept hot on a flat plate (see page 45).

To freeze ahead
This dish freezes for 2 months. Omit the eggs and cream until reheating the dish.

Salmis

This 'old-fashioned' term means a dish based upon lightly roasted poultry or game. This is carved or jointed, then put into an interesting sauce and heated; often additional ingredients are added. The Salmis can be served with the same accompaniments as when the poultry or game is served roasted. It is an ideal dish for a party; it looks elegant and can be prepared ahead.

Explicit recipes are unnecessary, for the choice of sauce is really unlimited. The Piquant Sauce on page 82, or the variations of gravy on page 89, are ideal. Make any sauce a little thinner than usual to compensate for evaporation during the heating period.

A Salmis of Duck and Prunes is particularly good. Joint the duck, make the Piquant Sauce, but omit the Worcestershire sauce. Add 175-225g (6-8oz) cooked prunes (for 4-6 people) plus a little prune syrup. If you make a Salmis of Pheasant or other game bird add cooked or canned chestnuts to the sauce.

Turkey à la King

Serves 8
100g (4oz) mushrooms
1 green pepper
50g (2oz) butter

For the sauce
50g (2oz) butter
50g (2oz) flour
300ml (½pt) milk
300ml (½pt) turkey stock
salt and pepper
2 eggs
150ml (¼pt) double cream

675g (1½lb) cooked turkey

To garnish
4 large slices bread
50g (2oz) butter
2tbspn chopped parsley

Variations
1 Use turkey fat in place of butter
2 Add about 100g (4oz) cooked or canned sweetcorn to the mixture
3 Add 2tbspn dry sherry with the egg and cream

Roast Meats

To many people a roast joint or roast poultry or game is one of the most enjoyable main courses. A disadvantage, though, in selecting this method of cooking for a dinner party is the feeling that you MUST dish-up at the last minute in order to maintain the good flavour, texture and appearance of the food. This is not the case if you follow the suggestions given on pages 42 to 44.

The table on page 90 indicates the average amount of meat etc to allow. It is generous if the food is preceded by very satisfying courses, but you may need to allow more if cold meat is to be left over for another meal, or if your family and friends have exceptionally large appetites.

The following points are worth considering:
Small turkeys or chickens have an excessively large proportion of bone to meat. If you do buy these, allow 50% more weight per person than the amount given in the table.
Goose tends to be extravagant, as the bone structure is so large. A 5.4kg (12lb) bird rarely serves more than 8 people.
Modern ducklings are being bred to give a greater yield of meat; a 1.75kg (4lb) bird would give generous portions for 2 people or smaller portions for 3.
Pheasant is an ideal choice if you are entertaining just one or two guests. A plump young pheasant yields generous portions for 2 people.
Grouse, on the other hand, has less meat and you need one small bird or half a larger bird per person.

Good Gravy

Many a perfect roast is spoiled by poor gravy. This sauce should be smooth as velvet, and full of flavour.

Make a generous amount of gravy, for it would be a problem if all your guests liked rather a lot and you found the supply running short. Allow at least 600ml (1pt) for 6 people.

For a thin gravy: Pour out all the dripping (fat) from the roasting tin except 1½tbspn. Leave in all those delicious little pieces of meat and stuffing that fall into the tin; these add flavour. If you prefer, spoon the 1½tbspn dripping, plus any residue from the roasting tin, into a saucepan. Blend 2 level tbspn flour into the fat; stir over a low heat until the flour turns a nutty brown colour. You can add a little gravy browning for extra colour. Gradually blend in 600ml (1pt) well-strained vegetable stock or stock from bones, poultry or game giblets.

Stir as the liquid comes to the boil, taste the gravy and adjust the seasoning; add any flavourings (see right). Strain into a heated sauce boat or keep hot until ready to serve.

For a thicker gravy: Use 40g (1½oz) flour to the proportions of dripping and liquid above.

Remember this recipe produces a good basic gravy; you can add flavourings to make it a super sauce.

To Flavour Gravy

Gravy should not be monotonous; it can be varied according to the meat or poultry with which it is being served. The following suggestions give interest to the basic recipes on the left.

Turkey, Chicken and Veal
Some stuffing generally falls into the tin, so this adds flavour. If you feel the gravy needs more interest, add a bouquet garni (removed when straining the gravy) and use a little white wine instead of all stock.

Pork, Duckling, Goose
These richer meats need a full-bodied gravy. Add a wineglass of port wine or red wine plus a shake of garlic salt and a few drops of Worcestershire sauce. A sliced onion could be roasted in the roasting tin with the meat or poultry.

Beef
Use a little red wine in the gravy plus 1tspn made mustard.

Lamb
A slightly sweet flavour is pleasant, so add 1tbspn of redcurrant jelly to the stock, together with a pinch of garlic salt.

Game
While you can add red wine, some old traditional recipes used some ale instead of all stock in the gravy and this gives a pleasant 'bite'. To balance this, add 1-2tbspn redcurrant jelly.

89

(opposite) Roast Duckling with Canned Peaches and Redcurrant Jelly

New Flavours For Roast Meats

Beef

1 Beef in Red Wine: Baste the meat with red wine as it cooks.
2 Add sliced onions to the tin during the cooking period; turn the beef several times.
3 Cut a joint of topside or boned and rolled sirloin downwards; sandwich the two halves with a Forcemeat stuffing (page 78), tie together, then roast.
4 Rub a little dry mustard powder, flour, salt and pepper into each side of the beef before roasting.

Lamb

1 Glazed Lamb: Pour away any fat from the tin 15 minutes before the end of the cooking time. Spread mint jelly over the joint, continue cooking.
2 Peel 1-2 garlic cloves, cut into thin slices (slivers). Insert under the skin of the lamb before roasting.
3 Colonial Goose: Use boned leg of lamb. Chop 125g (good 4oz) dried apricots, peel and grate a large onion, blend these with 125g (good 4oz) breadcrumbs, little chopped fresh or dried thyme, 25g (1oz) butter, 1tbspn clear honey, 1 egg, salt and pepper. Stuff the leg, tie securely and roast. See colour picture on page 80.
4 Crown Roast and Guard of Honour: The butcher will prepare these (given enough notice). In a Crown the two best ends (or a loin joint) are formed into a round. In the second joint the best ends are placed back to back with the tips crossed like swords. Stuffing can be inserted. Protect the bones with foil during roasting; garnish these with cutlet frills as shown in the colour picture on page 44.

Buying Meat etc for Roasting

Food	Minimum prepared weight per person	Usual accompaniments (see index for page numbers)
Turkey: dressed	450g (1lb) (see page 89)	Stuffings: Parsley and Thyme, Chestnut, Sausagemeat. Sauces: Bread, Cranberry. Thick gravy. Forcemeat Balls, Bacon rolls, Sausages.
Chicken	As Turkey	As Turkey
Goose	550-675g (1¼-1½lb) (see page 89)	Stuffings: Sage and Onion, Apple and Onion. Sauces: Apple (Cranberry or Orange also excellent). Thick gravy.
Grouse	Allow one small bird or half a larger bird per person	Fried Breadcrumbs, Game Chips (potato crisps), Bread Sauce and/or Redcurrant Jelly.
Duck	As Goose or allow one *small* Duckling to serve 2 people (see page 89)	As Goose
Beef: choose sirloin or rib	350g (12oz) if on bone; 225-300g (8-10oz) if boned	Yorkshire Pudding, Horseradish Sauce or Cream. Thin gravy.
Lamb: choose loin, saddle (double loin), leg or shoulder	As Beef	Redcurrant Jelly, Mint Sauce. Thin gravy.
Crown Roast or Guard of Honour	Allow 2-3 chops per person	Select any stuffing for these joints; you could serve thick gravy.
Pheasant	A plump bird serves 2-3	As Grouse
Pork	As Beef	As Goose or Duck
Veal	As Beef	As Turkey, although Cranberry Sauce is not a usual accompaniment
Venison	As Beef	As Pork

Preparing For Roasting

Always allow frozen poultry or game to defrost *completely* before roasting. It is a health hazard to try to roast these when semi-defrosted. As an example of the time needed for defrosting, a large turkey, over 8.1kg (18lb) in weight, needs 72 hours in the refrigerator or 30 hours in a cool place. I prefer to defrost meat also before it is roasted.

Poultry and game birds are lean and must therefore be given adequate additional fat, so keep the lean flesh well covered with plenty of fat bacon or butter. It is a good idea to cook turkey with the breast side downwards for half the total cooking period, then turn it the right way up. This gives a beautifully moist breast. Keep the bird well basted with the fat in the tin while cooking. If using foil, or a roaster bag for smaller birds, this stage is unnecessary. Open the foil for the last 30 minutes of cooking time, so the bird becomes really brown.

Goose or duck are fat birds, so you must allow any excess fat to run out. Stand on a trivet in the roasting tin. Do not wrap in foil or put into a roaster bag. Prick the skin lightly with a fine skewer after 30 minutes' cooking time and at regular intervals during cooking; you will see the fat spurt out.

Beef needs basting with a little fat from the tin during cooking. Beef is excellent if cooked in a covered roasting tin, in foil or a greased roaster bag. In this case, do not add extra fat. Too much fat in cooking beef tends to harden the outside.

Lamb generally has adequate fat and additional fat or basting is unnecessary.

Pork should be cooked to achieve the crisp crackling which is part of its appetising appearance and flavour. Make sure the skin is well chined (cut at regular intervals); brush this with oil or melted lard and add a light sprinkling of salt to encourage crisping. If you dislike excessive salt, omit this. Never cover pork when roasting.

Veal and venison are lean and the ideal preparation is to thread (lard) with fat pork or bacon. Cut the pork or bacon into narrow strips, put into a large larding needle and insert into the meat. Also keep the meat well basted with fat during cooking. Veal is particularly good when cooked in well-buttered foil or in a roaster bag.

Basting the meat during roasting means spooning the fat over from time to time; this helps to keep it moist. Roaster bags, foil and a proper covered roasting tin, where the splashing fat drops back again on to the meat, make basting unnecessary.

New Flavours for Roast Meats

Pork
1 Orange Pork: If roasting pork for 6-8 people, you need the juice of 2 large oranges, blended with 2 tbspn melted orange jelly marmalade and 1 crushed garlic clove. Cook the pork for the total time, less 15 minutes, then pour away all surplus fat. Spoon the orange mixture over the pork, complete cooking, baste at least twice with the mixture.
2 Cook sliced apples and onions with the pork. You need to roast the pork for half the time, then pour away all fat, add the apples and onions.
3 Pork, like lamb, is excellent with any fruit (see hints under Lamb, page 90).

Veal
Follow the suggestions under Poultry.

New Flavours For Roast Game

It is traditional to cover game with bacon instead of other fat, but chopped bacon can be put into birds before cooking. Another way to keep the birds moist is to place a knob of butter inside; this could be flavoured with chopped tarragon, rosemary or chervil.
1 Stuffed game birds: For each larger bird, such as pheasant, allow 50g (2oz) cream cheese mixed with 50g (2oz) skinned and deseeded grapes. Put into the bird before cooking. A little liver pâté can be used for a stuffing.
2 Baste the birds with Calvados (apple brandy) or Curaçao (orange brandy) during cooking.

New Flavours For Roast Poultry

Chicken or Turkey

1 Omit a stuffing, put a sprig of rosemary, 2-3 peeled potatoes and 25g (1oz) butter inside a chicken before cooking. Sieve and use as a thickening in the gravy.
2 Orange and Prunes: Squeeze orange juice over the bird before roasting. Serve with cooked prunes and fresh orange segments.
3 Tarragon and Cream Chicken: Put a sprig of tarragon into the bird before roasting. When almost cooked, spread double cream and chopped tarragon over the breast, complete cooking.
4 Brush the breast with honey and lemon juice just before the bird is quite cooked.
5 Roast peeled onions and dessert apples with the bird.
6 Baste the bird with white wine or cider (blended with a little brandy) or with apple or pineapple juice.

Duckling or Goose

1 Stuff the bird with soaked prunes and sliced dessert apples.
2 Duckling with Olives: Stuff each bird with 2-3tbspn sliced stuffed olives, 1 chopped raw onion and 25g (1oz) butter.
3 Duckling with Cherry Sauce: Blend 1tbspn duck fat with 150ml (¼pt) red wine, 150ml (¼pt) syrup from canned black or Morello cherries and 15g (½oz) cornflour. Cook until thickened and smooth. Add 225g (8oz) cherries and 2tbspn cherry brandy. Apricots or gooseberries could be used.

Timing For Roasting

Always calculate the cooking time *after* stuffing the joint or bird.

Two temperatures are given, No 1 and No 2. No 1 is for a moderately hot to hot oven and is therefore suitable for prime fresh poultry or sirloin of beef or first-class fresh pork.

Temperature No 2, which is very moderate to moderate, is the one to choose for defrosted frozen poultry or for defrosted meat or the less expensive cuts. If more convenient, you could select this lower temperature for all poultry and all meat, but I would *not* advise using Temperature 1 for any defrosted poultry or meat if you want it really tender.

You will notice I have given a slight range of settings in both Temperatures 1 and 2; this is because individual ovens vary a great deal. If you consider your oven slower than average, then use the higher setting; if, on the other hand, you think it is rather hotter than average, then use the lower one.

Temperature 1
Set the oven to 200-220°C, 400-425°F, Gas Mark 6-7. After cooking the poultry or a joint for an hour, reduce the heat to 190-200°C, 375-400°F, Gas Mark 5-6.
Allow:
Poultry and young Game Birds: 15 minutes per 450g (1lb) and 15 minutes over, up to 5.4kg (12lb) then 12 minutes per *additional* 450g (1lb).

Beef:
Rare — 15 minutes per 450g (1lb) and 15 minutes over.
Medium — 20 minutes per 450g (1lb) and 20 minutes over.

Lamb:
20 minutes per 450g (1lb) and 20 minutes over.

Pork, Veal and Venison:
25 minutes per 450g (1lb) and 25 minutes over.

Temperature 2
Set the oven to 160-180°C, 325-350°F, Gas Mark 3-4. Keep at this temperature throughout the cooking period.

Allow:
Poultry and young game birds: 22-25 minutes per 450g (1lb) and 22-25 minutes over, up to 5.4kg (12lb), then 20 minutes per *additional* 450g (1lb).

Beef:
Rare — 25 minutes per 450g (1lb) and 25 minutes over.
Medium — 30 minutes per 450g (1lb) and 30 minutes over.

Lamb:
35 minutes per 450g (1lb) and 35 minutes over.

Pork, Veal and Venison:
40 minutes per 450g (1lb) and 40 minutes over.

If using a covered roasting tin, allow an extra 10 minutes. If wrapping the bird or meat in foil, allow an extra 15-20 minutes cooking time. No extra time is required if using a roaster bag.
Note: If you intend the joint, poultry or game to be kept hot for at least an hour after cooking, under-cook by a total of 5-10 minutes.

(opposite) Roast Beef and Yorkshire Pudding, and Pavlva in a Hostess Royal trolley (see pages 82 and 107)

Carving

Good carving can be called an art; watch a skilled carver. The advice on page 18 stresses the importance of sharp knives, a proper carving fork and firm dish. Make sure the meat dish and serving plates are hot. It is an advantage for the cooked meat or poultry to stand for a while so that the flesh sets; this makes carving easier. If you have means of keeping the meat hot, eg in a Hostess heated trolley, it can stand for some time; if you are carving just after cooking, allow small joints and chickens to stand for at least 5 minutes, larger joints, or a turkey, at least 10-15 minutes; then start carving.

Bacon with Marinade Sauce

Serves 6
1.12-1.35kg (2½-3lb) collar of bacon
227g (8oz) can pineapple rings

For the marinade
6 juniper berries
150ml (¼pt) red wine
syrup from canned pineapple
4 tbspn red wine vinegar
1tbspn olive oil
1 bay leaf
black pepper

For the sauce and glaze
5tbspn demerara sugar
2tspn arrowroot
3tbspn water
1tspn Worcestershire sauce
2tspn tomato purée
½ green pepper

Variation
Gammon could be used; allow 25 minutes per 450g (1lb)

To Carve

If beef and veal are boned and rolled, carve slices across the meat. If carving rib of beef on the bone, carve from the outer edge of the meat towards the bone. Sirloin on the bone should be carved across the fillet, then the rib.

Cut leg of lamb towards the bone, then make a second cut to give a 'v' shaped slice; continue like this. Carve shoulder across and downwards, ie follow the contour of the shoulder bone. Crown Roast, Guard of Honour and loin of lamb are cut between the bones on a downwards movement.

As loin of pork is generally jointed and the fat scored to give good 'crackling', cut betweeen the bones. If boned and rolled, slice downwards. Carve leg as for lamb.

Small chickens, game birds and ducks are generally halved or cut into two leg and two breast and wing joints. Goose, larger chickens and turkey are always carved. To do this, first loosen one or both legs, then sever from the body. Carve slices from the breast and slices from the legs. Each person has some light (breast) meat and some dark (leg) meat, unless they express a preference for one or the other. Carve pheasant breast but serve leg joints.

Bacon with Marinade Sauce

Modern Danish bacon is mildly cured, so should not need soaking in water. Put the bacon into a closely-fitting bowl. Crush the juniper berries, mix with the marinade ingredients; pour over the bacon, leave for 24 hours, turning the joint once or twice.

Remove the bacon from the marinade, wrap loosely in foil, roast in the centre of a moderate oven, 190°C, 375°F, Gas Mark 5; allow 35 minutes per 450g (1lb) but deduct 20 minutes from the total time. At the end of the roasting period remove the bacon from the oven, unwrap, cut away the skin, score the fat. Coat with 2tbspn of the sugar. Return to the oven, raising the heat to moderately hot, 200°C, 400°F, Gas Mark 6. Do not cover the bacon as the sugar should glaze this.

Meanwhile strain the marinade into a saucepan. Blend the arrowroot with the water, add to the marinade with the sauce, purée and remaining 3tbspn of the sugar. Bring to the boil, stir until thickened. Dice and blanch the pepper for 5 minutes in boiling water. Reserve three pineapple rings, chop the remainder of the fruit, add the pepper and chopped pineapple to the sauce. Garnish the bacon and dish with pineapple rings. Serve with Duchesse potatoes (see picture page 81) and the sauce.

To keep the food hot
Follow the directions under 'Meat and Poultry Dishes' on page 43; do not cover.

To freeze ahead
Do not freeze the cooked dish or sauce.

Frikadeller

Put the beef and pork through a fine mincer. Peel and mince or grate the onion. Mix the meat with the flour, salt, pepper and allspice, add the onion. Stir in the milk and egg. Using two dessertspoons and a little melted butter, shape the mixture into oblong balls. Melt the butter in a frying pan and gently fry the Frikadeller until brown on both sides; drain.

Serve hot with Caramelised Potatoes and Carrots (page 55), or cold with salad. See colour picture on page 49.

To keep the food hot
Spoon the Meat Balls on to absorbent paper or a heated serving dish. Place into the hot cupboard of a Hostess trolley or cabinet or on a heat tray or in a cool oven. Do not cover.

To freeze ahead
These freeze very well. Cool after frying, open-freeze then pack. Use within 3 months. To reheat, either toss in a little hot butter in a frying pan or lay on a flat dish and reheat in the oven.

Turkey and Walnut Croquettes

Mince the cooked turkey very finely; chop the walnuts. Melt the fat, butter or margarine, add the flour and cook for a few minutes over a low heat. Remove from the heat, gradually add the milk, salt and pepper to taste. Bring the sauce to the boil, stir over a low heat as the mixture thickens. Allow to cool. Add the turkey meat, walnuts, parsley, herbs and lemon or orange rind. Mix together thoroughly; adjust the seasoning if necessary. Smooth the mixture out on a plate and stand in the refrigerator to cool; it then becomes more manageable. Divide into 8 good-sized portions as shown in the colour picture on page 15, or 16-24 smaller-sized pieces. Form into round and fairly flat cakes. Blend a little salt and pepper with the flour, put this on to a piece of greaseproof paper, or into a large greaseproof or polythene bag. Coat the croquettes in the seasoned flour. Beat the eggs, brush over the croquettes then coat in the breadcrumbs. These are easier to cook if deep-fried in hot oil, but they can be shallow-fried in a little heated oil in a frying pan until crisp and golden. Drain well on absorbent paper. Serve hot or cold, garnished with sprigs of parsley and tomato water-lilies. See colour picture on page 15.

To keep the food hot
These croquettes are equally good hot or cold. If you decide to serve them hot, place the croquettes on a thick layer of absorbent paper or a savoury doyley and keep hot in the cupboard of a Hostess trolley or cabinet, on a heat tray or in a cool oven. Do not cover.

To freeze ahead
Cook, cool, open-freeze then wrap. Use within 3 months.

Frikadeller

Serves 6-8
350g (12oz) lean beef
350g (12oz) lean pork
1 small onion
25g (1oz) flour
½tspn salt
¼tspn pepper
¾tspn ground allspice
180ml (6 fl oz) milk
1 egg
little melted butter

For frying
75g (3oz) butter

Variation
To make a richer mixture blend with double cream instead of milk

Turkey and Walnut Croquettes

Serves 8
For the croquettes
900g (2lb) cooked turkey meat
50g (2oz) walnuts
225g (8oz) turkey fat, butter or margarine
225g (8oz) flour
1.2L (2pt) milk
salt and black pepper
2tbspn chopped parsley
2tbspn chopped fresh herbs (use chives, thyme or basil or a mixture of herbs)
1tbspn finely grated lemon or orange rind (optional)

For coating
40g (1½oz) flour
2 eggs
approximately 75g (3oz) crisp breadcrumbs

For frying
oil

To garnish
parsley
tomatoes

95

Cooking Vegetables

The golden rule is not to over-cook vegetables. If they are cooked for too long a period they lose colour and texture as well as flavour. This is particularly important when you intend to keep the vegetables hot. See page 43. Green vegetables should be put into the minimum quantity of boiling salted water and cooked as quickly as possible with the lid on the saucepan.

Remember that frozen vegetables have been partly cooked when 'blanched' before freezing, so it is essential to time the cooking carefully. Canned vegetables have been pre-cooked so only require heating.

When roasting potatoes make sure they are rolled in hot fat as soon as they are put into the tin. This prevents any possibility of the vegetables discolouring before they start to brown. It is a good idea to make them extra crisp if you intend to keep them waiting in which case serve on a flat uncovered dish; condensation would soften the potatoes if placed in a covered vegetable or Hostess dish.

Serving Vegetables

Plan the selection of vegetables to give a really good combination of colours as well as flavours. The pictures on pages 53, 93 and 97 illustrate this point well.

Introduce extra colour in the form of diced red and green peppers, tomatoes and parsley if you feel your choice of vegetables provides plenty of flavour but little colour.

Vegetables

The following vegetables retain texture, flavour and colour even when dished-up well ahead of the meal. It is, however, important to follow the advice on page 43 for keeping vegetables hot. Remember to toss the cooked and well-strained vegetables in melted butter or margarine before placing into the dishes.

Asparagus or globe artichokes should be prepared and cooked as on page 62. If serving with the main course, provide an extra plate for each diner as these vegetables are spoiled when covered with gravy or a strongly-flavoured sauce on the dinner plate. Serve with hot butter or Hollandaise or Mousseline Sauce, as the recipes on page 79. Top asparagus with finely grated cheese or the Polonaise topping given for cauliflower below.

Beans, broad and green, are delicious if lightly cooked, strained, then blended with melted butter and skinned, diced, or sliced, fresh tomatoes, chopped parsley and chives. Toss over the heat for a few minutes but do not overcook the tomatoes.

Broccoli and cauliflower can be topped with Cheese or Hollandaise Sauce (recipes page 79), or with fried breadcrumbs, chopped hard-boiled eggs and parsley (known as Polonaise).

Carrots and other root vegetables look colourful and more interesting if cooked, strained, then blended with chopped crisply-fried bacon and fried onion rings. These vegetables can be blended with Parsley Sauce, (page 79) or cooked in well-seasoned tomato juice instead of water.

Courgettes and aubergines are essential ingredients for Ratatouille (page 62) but these vegetables can be sliced and simmered in well-seasoned tomato juice or stock until tender and all the surplus moisture has been absorbed. Add a generous amount of chopped parsley and chives.

Peas have a more subtle flavour if cooked with a few whole spring onions, or thinly sliced onions, and sliced mushrooms. Use the minimum amount of salted water plus a generous knob of butter so the liquid is absorbed by the time the peas are tender.

Potatoes look attractive if served Duchesse style, shown in the picture on page 81. Cook and mash the potatoes until very smooth. Do not add milk. To each 450g (1lb) potatoes add 50g (2oz) butter, 2 egg yolks, salt and pepper to taste. Pipe into attractive shapes and brown in the oven. Duchesse potatoes freeze well for several months.

Roast potatoes seem the perfect accompaniment to roast joints or poultry; do not ignore sweet potatoes or yams. These are obtainable from most good greengrocers at various periods of the year. They are particularly good with roast turkey or game. Peel, cut into portions and roast as ordinary potatoes, but allow a slightly shorter cooking time as the sugar content causes them to burn rather easily.

(opposite) Trout with Dijon Sauce and Selection of Vegetables in a Hostess Carousel (see page 75)

Flavourings for an Omelette

Add chopped fresh herbs or 25-50g (1-2oz) grated cheese or fried sliced mushrooms to the egg before cooking.

Fill the omelette with Cheese Sauce and/or cooked vegetables such as asparagus, spinach or tomatoes.

Quiche aux Champignons

Gives 8-10 small portions
short crust pastry made with 225g (8oz) flour, etc (page 109)

For the filling
350g (12oz) mushrooms
50g (2oz) butter
225g (8oz) Gruyère or Cheddar cheese
25g (1oz) Parmesan cheese (optional)
3 whole eggs
3 egg yolks
300ml (½pt) milk
450ml (¾pt) single cream
salt and pepper

Variations
1 French Onion Tart: Use 675g (1½lb) thinly sliced onions and 1-2 garlic cloves instead of mushrooms
2 Quiche aux Légumes: Use a selection of cooked vegetables
3 Quiche aux Poissons: Use cooked shell or other fish instead of mushrooms
4 Quiche au Jambon or Quiche Lorraine: Use cooked, diced ham or fried chopped bacon

For Vegetarians

As most vegetarians are cheese-eaters, one of the simplest ways to add extra food value to their meal is to serve bowls of grated cheese and chopped nuts to sprinkle over vegetables or salads. A Cheese Sauce (recipe on page 79) can turn hard-boiled eggs, or a selection of vegetables, into a satisfying and sustaining dish. An omelette is a good egg dish. The cooking time for this is so brief that, if you have all the ingredients ready, you will not need to leave your guests for more than a few minutes. The Quiche on this page would be equally popular with vegetarians (providing you use the basic recipe, or variations 1 or 2) or with non-vegetarians.

Omelettes

Prepare any fillings or flavourings (see left-hand column). To make a medium-sized omelette for one person, beat 2-3 eggs with a fork, add a little salt and pepper. Heat 25g (1oz) butter in a small omelette pan, pour in the eggs, leave for about half a minute, or until the eggs begin to set. Tilt the pan so the liquid egg runs to the side of the pan, continue cooking as quickly as possible. Add any filling, fold the omelette away from the handle, tip on to a hot plate and serve at once.

Quiche aux Champignons

This is an excellent dish for vegetarians, but as a quiche is so popular, it can be served to all your guests.

Roll out the pastry and line a flan dish or tin of approximately 25-26cm (10-10½in) in diameter and at least 3.5cm (1½in) in depth. Bake 'blind' for 15 minutes in the centre of a moderately hot oven, 200°C, 400°F, Gas Mark 6, or until the pastry is set but not yet golden. Meanwhile wipe and thinly slice the mushrooms; heat the butter and cook the mushrooms until just tender. Grate the cheese(s). Spoon the mushrooms and cheese into the pastry case. Beat the eggs and egg yolks, warm the milk and pour over the eggs, add the cream, salt and pepper to taste, then strain into the pastry case. Return the quiche to the centre of the oven, lowering the heat to very moderate, 160°C, 325°F, Gas Mark 3, for 45 minutes, or to slow, 150°C, 300°F, Gas Mark 2, for an hour or until set.

To keep the food hot
As the egg custard filling would spoil with too much heat, put in a *very* slow oven or in the hot cupboard of the Hostess trolley or cabinet or on a heat tray. Do not cover.

To freeze ahead
Cook, then cool the quiche, freeze then wrap. This can be stored for 3 months. Reheat gently from the frozen state.

Interesting Salads

Salads should look as good as they taste and a selection of salads is ideal for a buffet; one or more salads can be served as an accompaniment to hot as well as cold dishes.

Prepare salad ingredients carefully; wash, shake or pat dry and store in a covered container in the refrigerator. Ready-prepared salads should be lightly covered with clingfilm or foil so they keep crisp and moist. Do not add any oil and vinegar dressing to green or mixed salads until ready to serve, as this causes the lettuce etc to become limp.

A green salad is made from the ingredients in the adjoining column, whereas a mixed salad adds more colourful ingredients, such as tomatoes, radishes, sliced hard-boiled eggs, etc. Be adventurous, though, with salads; add fruit in season to the more usual vegetables; use raw cauliflower and peppers for winter salads (picture page 15).

Russian Salad
Dice then cook the fresh or frozen vegetables, drain and mix with Mayonnaise while warm; cool and add finely chopped parsley. A little grated onion or chopped spring onions helps to give more taste to this rather bland salad.

The original recipes for Russian salad often included chopped hard-boiled eggs and diced tongue, so you may like to return to the classic recipe.

Spanish Rice Salad
Cook the rice as page 114, drain and blend with the Mayonnaise while still warm, then allow to cool. Add all or some of the salad ingredients suggested in the adjoining column. Instead of Mayonnaise you could mix the rice with yoghurt and lemon juice.

Crunchy Chicken Salad

Put the red and green peppers into boiling water for 4-5 minutes and simmer for 4 minutes only. This process 'blanches' the peppers, softens the flesh slightly but does not destroy either the colour or texture. Cut the peppers into neat slices, discard the cores and seeds. Divide the cauliflower into florets. Wipe the courgettes, slice neatly; chop the celery and slice the radishes. Lift the pineapple out of the syrup, cut the rings into squares. Dice the chicken. In a large bowl, mix together the chicken, peppers, cauliflower, courgettes, celery, radishes and pineapple. Put all the ingredients for the dressing into a screw-top jar and shake well. Blend the dressing with the salad ingredients about 30 minutes before serving. Top with the chopped parsley. See colour illustration on page 15.

To freeze ahead
This is an excellent salad in which to use defrosted frozen chicken.

Green Salad
This can include lettuce or endive, green pepper, cucumber, watercress, chicory. It is tossed in an oil and vinegar dressing, ie French or Vinaigrette Dressing.

Russian Salad
Use carrots, turnips, swedes, potatoes, French or runner beans and peas, with Mayonnaise.

Spanish Rice Salad
Allow 25g (1oz) rice per person and 1-2tbspn Mayonnaise. Add cooked mixed vegetables or grated raw carrots; chopped celery, cucumber; diced peppers; diced skinned tomatoes.

Crunchy Chicken Salad

Serves 6
1 red pepper
1 green pepper
½ small cauliflower
2 courgettes
2 sticks celery
6-8 radishes
2 rings canned pineapple
450g (1lb) cooked chicken

For the dressing
1tbspn white wine vinegar
3tbspn olive oil
salt and black pepper
pinch dry mustard

To garnish
1tbspn chopped parsley

Danish Buttercream

Put 150ml (¼pt) milk and 110g (4oz) unsalted butter into a saucepan. Heat gently until the butter has melted. Soften ½tspn gelatine in 2tspn cold water. Pour a little of the hot milk and butter mixture over the gelatine, stir well, then tip into the saucepan with the remaining butter and milk. Add 1-2tspn sugar, stir over the heat for 1 minute to make sure the gelatine is perfectly dissolved. Pour this mixture into a liquidiser goblet and mix at maximum speed for 30 seconds, then pour into a basin, cover and leave in the refrigerator for several hours. Whip to a spreading consistency.

To decorate the Gâteau

Serves 8-10
Whip 450ml (¾pt) double cream, whip in 3-4tbspn milk. Open 1 or 2 425g (15oz) can(s) black cherries; drain. Grate 110g (4oz) chocolate. Cut the cake into 3 layers, spread the first layer with cherry jam, moisten with a little Kirsch, cherry brandy or cherry syrup. Spread with cherries and cream. Put on the second layer, repeat this process. Top with the final layer of cake. Coat the whole cake with cream, pipe rosettes of cream on top. Press the grated chocolate against the sides and top of the cake. Decorate with halved grapes or cherries.

Puddings and Desserts

The recipes in this section range from traditional Christmas Pudding to light frozen or chilled desserts.

Some of the most popular desserts of today are light gâteaux; these are equally suitable for a dinner, luncheon or buffet party or to serve with tea or coffee.

Redcurrant Layer Gâteau

Prepare the Danish Buttercream first, to allow time for it to set; the recipe is on the left. You could use all whipped cream for the filling if preferred. Buy 550g (1¼lb) redcurrants. Grease and flour or line two 20cm (8in) sandwich tins.

To prepare the Victoria Sponge mixture, cream 175g (6oz) butter with 175g (6oz) caster sugar. Gradually beat in 3 large eggs. Sieve 175g (6oz) self-raising flour, or plain flour and 1½tspn baking powder, fold carefully into the creamed mixture. Divide the mixture between the two tins. Bake for 18-20 minutes, or until firm to the touch, just above the centre of a moderate oven, 180-190°C, 350-375°F, Gas Mark 4-5. Turn out and allow to cool. Cut each sponge in half, so giving 4 layers.

Crush about 350g (12oz) of the redcurrants with a little sugar. Sandwich the layers of sponge with the mashed fruit and the Danish Buttercream filling. Whip 150ml (¼pt) double or whipping cream, add a little sugar, spread over the cake, then top with the whole fruit and a light sprinkling of sugar.

Any seasonal fruit could be used instead of redcurrants.

Black Forest Gâteau

There are many versions of this very well-known gâteau. The simplest is to adapt the sponge recipe above, ie omit 25g (1oz) flour and use 25g (1oz) cocoa powder instead. There is, however, a much more interesting mixture you could use for the cake illustrated on page 101.

Line a 20-23cm (8-9in) cake tin with greased greaseproof paper. Melt 150g (5oz) plain chocolate in 1tbspn of water. Cream together 150g (5oz) butter, 150g (5oz) sieved icing sugar, add the yolks of 5 eggs and the melted chocolate. Sieve 150g (5oz) self-raising flour, or 150g (5oz) plain flour with 1tspn baking powder, and 25g (1oz) of cornflour. Fold into the creamed mixture. Whisk the egg whites until they hold their shape, but do not over-whisk. Fold into the chocolate mixture. Spoon into the cake tin. Bake for 50 minutes or until firm to the touch in the centre of a slow oven, 150°C, 300°F, Gas Mark 2. Cool in the tin for 5 minutes, turn out carefully and complete the gâteau as on the left. See colour picture opposite.

(opposite above) Black Forest Gâteau

(opposite below) Dutch Ginger Shortcake (see above and page 119)

Sizes of Basins to Choose

Use 2 2L (3½pt) basins; each gives generous portions for 8 people
or
4 1L (1¾pt) basins; each gives generous portions for 4 people.

To Cook a Christmas Pudding

Steam each of the 2L (3½pt) puddings for 6-7 hours or the 1L (1¾pt) puddings for 4-5 hours, or allow 1-2 hours in a pressure cooker at H/15lb pressure. If you have no steamer, stand the basins on an upturned saucer or patty tin in a saucepan of water, so the water only comes halfway up the basin. Keep the liquid boiling fairly steadily; always top up with boiling water. On Christmas Day, re-steam for 2-3 hours or allow 30 minutes at H/15lb in a pressure cooker.

Mince Pies

Use double the amount of flan (fleur) pastry (page 109) and about 450g (1lb) mincemeat for 18-24 mince pies.
Line patty tins with rounds of pastry, fill with mincemeat; moisten the edges of the pastry. Top with smaller rounds of pastry for the 'lids'; make slits on top with scissors. Bake for 20 minutes in the centre of a moderate to moderately hot oven, 190-200°C, 375-400°F, Gas Mark 5-6.
A large mince tart, as shown in the colour picture on page 53 should be baked for approximately 30 minutes; reduce the heat slightly after 20 minutes.

Christmas Pudding

Sieve 110g (4oz) plain or self-raising flour with ½tspn each of ground cinnamon, ground nutmeg, powdered mace and allspice. Chop 110g (4oz) glacé cherries, 110g (4oz) dried apricots, 110g (4oz) prunes, 175g (6oz) candied peel and 110g (4oz) blanched almonds. Peel and finely grate 1 medium carrot; peel and coarsely grate 1 large cooking apple. Grate the rind from 1 lemon and 1 orange. Mix all these ingredients together. Add 175g (6oz) currants, 350g (12oz) sultanas, 560g (1¼lb) raisins, 225g (8oz) soft breadcrumbs, 225g (8oz) brown sugar, 175g (6oz) shredded suet or melted butter, 2 level tbspn golden syrup, 275ml (scant ½pt) beer, 4 eggs and 2tbspn sweet sherry. Mix all the ingredients together, stir very well. For a more moist pudding, add the juice of the lemon and orange. Let the mixture stand overnight to mature in flavour.

Grease and flour two large or four smaller pudding basins (see left). Fill the basins to within 2.5cm (1in) of the top. Cover with greaseproof paper. Cook as on the left. When cooked, remove damp covers. Cool the puddings, put on dry covers and store in a cool, dry place.

To keep the food hot
Turn the pudding out of the basin on to a hot serving dish, cover lightly with foil or replace the basin to ensure the outside of the pudding does not dry. Keep hot in a low oven, over a pan of boiling water or in the hot cupboard of a Hostess trolley.

To freeze ahead
Cook, cool, then freeze, if you are worried about storage conditions. The flavour matures better at room temperature.

Mincemeat

Peel and core 1 medium cooking apple and grate coarsely. Grate the rind from 1 large lemon and squeeze out the juice. Chop 110g (4oz) candied peel and 110g (4oz) blanched almonds, mix with the apple and lemon rind and juice, then add the following: 450g (1lb) mixed dried fruit, 110g (4oz) shredded suet or melted margarine, 110g (4oz) sugar, preferably demerara, 1tspn mixed spice, ½tspn each of ground cinnamon and grated nutmeg, 4tbspn brandy, whisky or rum. Mix together thoroughly, put into dry jam jars and cover well. Store in a cool, dry place. Makes good 1kg (2¼-2½lb).

Crêpes Suzette

Sieve the flour and salt into a bowl, gradually beat in the eggs, then the milk and water. Add the oil or melted butter just before cooking (this helps to give a crisper texture to the pancakes). To cook the pancakes, heat a little oil, fat or butter in a pan, then pour in sufficient batter to give a wafer-thin coating — many people use too much batter and so have a solid pancake. Cook steadily until crisp and golden brown — this takes 1-2 minutes — then turn or toss and cook for the same time on the second side. Keep warm while cooking the remaining pancakes. To make the filling, cream together the butter and sugar, then add the grated orange or tangerine rind and Curaçao. Place some filling in each pancake, fold in four. Pour the orange or tangerine juice into a large frying pan with sugar to taste, then add the pancakes and allow the liquid to simmer gently for a few minutes. Finally add the Curaçao, heat thoroughly and ignite if desired.

To keep the food hot
Do not ignite the sauce before keeping hot, save this for the finishing touch. Keep in the dish of a Hostess trolley or cabinet or a tightly covered dish on a heat tray or in a very cool oven.

To freeze ahead
The dish freezes well for 3 months but the Curaçao tends to lose its potency so it is advisable to add this liqueur when reheating.

Freezing pancakes
Plain unfilled pancakes freeze well, especially if the oil or butter is added to the batter. Separate each with oiled greaseproof paper.

Pineapple Nougat

Put the nuts on a metal plate and toast under the grill until golden. Cut the angelica into leaf shapes (see picture on page 30). Reserve one pineapple ring, cherry and a little angelica with a few nuts for decoration. Drain and chop the remaining pineapple rings, cherries and angelica into small pieces. Put about one-third of this mixture on one side for decoration. Cut each marshmallow into small pieces (with scissors dipped in pineapple juice). Mix the marshmallows with the remaining pineapple, cherries, nuts and the lemon juice. Whip the cream until it holds its shape. Spoon a little into a piping bag with a star nozzle, blend the remainder with the marshmallow mixture. Spoon into a serving dish. Slice the reserved pineapple ring thinly to make two rings. Cut each through the centre, make two twists and place on the dessert. Pipe a star of cream in each cone. Decorate with a quarter of a cherry and a piece of angelica. Spoon the remaining mixture round the edge of the dish. Chill for several hours or overnight if possible.

To freeze ahead
This sweet can be kept in the freezing compartment of a refrigerator for a few days. For long-term storage keep in an airtight container in a deep freeze. It may be served iced (as ice cream) or allowed to thaw.

Crêpes Suzette

Serves 4-6
For the batter
100g (4oz) plain flour
pinch salt
2 eggs
250ml (scant ½pt) milk and water
½tbspn oil or melted butter

For frying
oil, fat or butter

For the filling
100g (4oz) butter
75-100g (3-4oz) sugar
grated rind of 2 oranges or 3 tangerines
1tbspn Curaçao

For the sauce
150ml (¼pt) orange or tangerine juice
sugar to taste
2-3tbspn Curaçao

Variation
To give more interest to the sauce heat 25g (1oz) butter with 50g (2oz) caster sugar until pale golden brown, then add the orange or tangerine juice and heat gently.
Finally add the Curaçao as the basic recipe

Pineapple Nougat

Serves 8-10
25g (1oz) finely chopped almond nibs
small piece of angelica
435g (15½oz) can pineapple rings
50g (2oz) glacé cherries
225g (8oz) marshmallows
2tbspn lemon juice
600ml (1pt) double cream

Variation
Add 50g (2oz) sugar to the whipped cream

103

Ice Cream

Serves 8-12
150g (5oz) caster sugar
5 large eggs
600ml (1pt) double or whipping
  cream or use half double and
  half single cream

Flavourings
1 Use ½-1tspn vanilla or other
essence
2 Coffee: Dissolve 1-1½tbspn
instant coffee in 3tbspn hot
milk; cool, blend with the
cream mixture before freezing
3 Chocolate: Melt 100g (4oz)
plain chocolate, cool and blend
with the cream mixture before
freezing
4 Fruit: Blend 300ml (½pt)
smooth thick fruit purée into
the cream mixture when
half-frozen. Choose apple,
berry fruits, mango, melon,
plum, rhubarb, etc. Check
sweetness of mixture
5 Lemon: Freeze mixture until
slightly thickened, fold in the
sieved pulp of 2 large lemons
and ½-1tspn grated lemon
'zest' plus a little extra sugar
6 Liqueur: Add 4tbspn of your
favourite liqueur to the
half-frozen ice cream. Be a little
sparing with the sugar as
liqueurs are sweet *and too much
sugar prevents freezing*
7 Rum and Chocolate: Soak 50g
(2oz) seedless raisins in 2tbspn
rum for 1-2 hours. Chop 100g
(4oz) *crisp* after-dinner
chocolate mints into small
pieces. Add to the half-frozen
ice cream
8 Sicilian: Blend 100g (4oz)
chopped Maraschino cherries,
50g (2oz) chopped nuts, 25g
(1oz) diced angelica and 50g
(2oz) coarsely broken ratafias
(recipe page 106) with the
cream mixture before freezing.
A little dried fruit could also be
added

Ice cream

Whisk the sugar and eggs until thick and creamy. Whip the cream in a separate bowl (do not overbeat) or whip the double cream, then gradually whisk in the single cream. Add any flavouring required and place in the freezing compartment of the refrigerator, or into the freezer. Whisking and stirring is not necessary with this particular recipe, unless you add heavy fruit and nuts (as in Sicilian). In this case the ice cream should be stirred when almost frozen to distribute the fruit. The number of portions depends upon the other foods served with the ice cream.

This ice cream keeps for up to 3 months in a freezer.

Sorbets

Select fruit with a refreshing flavour, such as apple, berry fruits, blackcurrants, orange, rhubarb, etc. Sieve or liquidise the fruit to give a smooth purée, or use fruit juice. Orange, pineapple or other fruit juices can be used undiluted, but lemon is so strong it is better to add some water. Sweeten the purée or juice to taste, but do not make over-sweet.

To 900ml (1½pt) purée or juice allow 1½tspn gelatine and 4-6 egg whites. Soften, then dissolve the gelatine in a little purée or juice, add to the remainder of the purée or juice. Freeze until the consistency of soft whipped cream. Whisk the egg whites until stiff, fold into the mixture. Continue freezing. Use within 3 months.

Serve in chilled glasses or lemon or orange peel cases.

Vanilla Cheesecake

Crush 175g (6oz) digestive biscuits. Melt 50g (2oz) butter, add to the biscuits with 50g (2oz) caster sugar. Butter the inside of a 20-23cm (8-9in) cake tin with a loose base. Press the biscuit crumb mixture on to the base and sides of the tin.

Cream 75g (3oz) butter with 75g (3oz) caster sugar and ½tspn vanilla essence. Separate the whites from the yolks of 3 eggs; beat the yolks into the creamed mixture, then add 450g (1lb) cream cheese and 3tbspn double cream, blend thoroughly. Whisk the egg whites, fold into the cheese mixture.

Bake the cheesecake in the centre of a cool oven, 150°C, 300°F, Gas Mark 2 for 1-1¼ hours until just firm. Cool in the oven with the door left open; when quite cold remove from the tin.

Like all cheesecakes it freezes well for 3 months. This can be topped with whipped cream and seasonal fruit. As this is both substantial and rich it should serve up to 8.

Lemon Syllabub

Rub the sugar over the lemon rind to extract the flavour and remove the yellow-coloured 'zest'. Put the sugar into a basin. Halve 2-3 of the lemons, squeeze out enough juice to give 4tbspn. Add to the sugar, crush this, then leave standing for a time, to allow the sugar to dissolve. Whip the double cream until firm, gradually add the single cream, whisking briskly as you do so. Whisk in the lemon and sugar mixture. Finally add the brandy or sherry. Spoon into small glasses and chill well. Serve with sweet biscuits.

To freeze ahead
Do not freeze this mixture.

Apricot Brandy Coronet

Open the canned fruit, drain well and reserve 150ml (¼pt) syrup from the can. Put the marshmallows, brandy and reserved syrup into a saucepan, dissolve over a low heat. When completely dissolved, cool until the mixture begins to thicken. Rinse a 0.75L (1½pt) fluted jelly mould in cold water or brush with 2-3 drops oil. Whip the cream until it holds its shape, then fold three-quarters into the marshmallow mixture. Reserve 4 apricot halves for decoration, chop the remainder. Add the chopped apricots to the cream mixture, spoon into the mould and chill overnight in the refrigerator. Unmould on to the serving dish. Pipe a little cream on the sides of the mould and press brandy snaps against this. Top with more cream and the halved apricots. See colour picture on page 27.

To freeze ahead
This dessert can be frozen and served as ice cream. Add the brandy snaps at the last minute.

Traditional Tipsy Cake

Cut the sponge cake into 4 layers. It is easier to split this cake if slightly stale. It is traditional to use 3 different jams in this dessert. Put the first layer of sponge on to a serving dish. Spread with raspberry jam, moisten with a little sherry and wine (sherry only could be used). Add the second layer of sponge, spread with apricot jam and moisten with the alcohol. Place the third layer of sponge in position, spread with greengage jam, add the alcohol. Allow to stand for several hours. Whip the cream until it just holds its shape, add the sugar, spread over the top and sides of the cake, then add the decorations.

Lemon Syllabub

Serves 8-10
100g (4oz) loaf sugar
4 lemons
600ml (1pt) double cream
600ml (1pt) single cream
4tbspn brandy or sherry

Apricot Brandy Coronet

Serves 8
435g (15½oz) can apricot
    halves
175g (6oz) marshmallows
3tbspn brandy
300ml (½pt) double cream
8 brandy snaps

Traditional Tipsy Cake

Serves 8
Victoria sponge cake as page
    100
raspberry, apricot and
    greengage jam
at least 150 ml (¼pt) sweet
    sherry
at least 150ml (¼pt) sweet
    white wine
300ml (½pt) double cream
25g (1oz) sugar

To decorate
few ratafias
glacé or Maraschino cherries
piece of angelica
25-50g (1-2oz) blanched flaked
    almonds

Mont Blanc

Serves 8-10
425g (15oz) can unsweetened
    chestnut purée
few drops vanilla essence
50g (2oz) caster sugar

To decorate
icing sugar

Traditional Trifle

Serves 8-10
For the custard sauce
900ml (1½pt) milk
5 egg yolks or 3 large eggs
50-75g (2-3oz) sugar
vanilla pod or a few drops
    vanilla essence

6 trifle sponge cakes
apricot jam
3-4tbspn sherry
40g (1½oz) blanched split
    almonds

To decorate
300ml (½pt) double cream
few glacé or Maraschino
    cherries
angelica
ratafias
50-75g (2-3oz) blanched
    almonds

Variations
1 Use half milk and half single
cream in the custard
2 Add a layer of drained canned
fruit over the sponge cakes;
pears, peaches, lychees are
particularly suitable
3 Scottish Trifle: Moisten the
sponge cakes with white wine
plus a dash of whisky instead of
sherry
4 Non-alcoholic Trifle: Moisten
the sponge cakes with canned or
cooked fruit syrup, flavoured
with a little orange juice

Mont Blanc

Put the chestnut purée into a basin, add the vanilla and sugar. Blend, but do not over-beat, as the mixture must not be sticky. Spoon into a large piping bag with a No 3 writing pipe. Pipe into a pyramid shape on the serving plate. Sieve the icing sugar over the top. Serve with well-chilled single or double cream.

To freeze ahead
This can be frozen for 3 months. Dust with the icing sugar after defrosting.

Traditional Trifle

For special occasions, prepare a *real* egg custard, although you can use custard powder. As an egg custard takes time to cook, prepare first. Warm the milk; beat the egg yolks or eggs with the sugar, add the milk and vanilla pod or essence and cook very slowly in a double saucepan or a basin over hot water until thickened. Split the sponge cakes, sandwich with the jam, put into a large serving dish or individual dishes. Soak in the sherry and top with the blanched almonds. Pour the hot custard over the sponge cakes, cover with a plate to prevent a skin forming on the custard. Allow to cool. Whip the cream until it holds its shape; spread a layer over the custard, then use the remainder to pipe the decoration. Top with the glacé or Maraschino cherries, angelica cut into leaf shapes, ratafia biscuits and blanched almonds. The almonds can be browned under the grill or in the oven.

To freeze ahead
Trifles do not freeze well, unless the custard is made with cream and milk (see Variation 1).

Ratafias

These tiny macaroons are easily made if you cannot buy them at the grocers; they generally are sold in packets. They keep well in the freezer or an airtight tin.

Whisk 2 egg whites until frothy. Add 150g (5oz) caster sugar and 150g (5oz) ground almonds, plus a few drops of almond essence. Put tiny balls the size of a pea on rice paper or a greased baking tray. Bake for 5-8 minutes in the centre of a very moderate oven, 160°C, 325°F, Gas Mark 3. Makes about 60.

Crème Caramel

Put the sugar and 5tbspn water into a strong saucepan; stir until the sugar has dissolved; boil steadily until a golden-brown caramel. Add last 1tbspn water, stir until blended then pour into a 1.25L (generous 2pt) oven-proof mould or tin, turn to coat the sides and bottom of the container; allow to cool and stiffen.

Beat the egg yolks, or whole eggs and yolks with the sugar. Warm the milk and/or cream, pour over the whisked egg mixture, cool then strain into the mould. Stand the container in a 'bain-marie' (see page 45). Bake in the centre of a slow oven, 140-150°C, 275-300°F, Gas Mark 1-2 for 1½-2 hours or until firm. Cool slightly, unmould on to the serving dish.

To freeze ahead
Do not freeze unless using cream. Serve within a month. Make the custard for the Crème Brûlée in the same way; freeze without the topping. Add this when the custard has defrosted.

Pavlova

Use either a silicone baking tray or place silicone (non-stick) paper on the tray or oil a baking tray lightly, or draw on greaseproof paper an oval or round 20cm (8in) in diameter. Place on a greased baking tray and oil the paper well. Whisk the egg whites and vanilla essence until stiff. Sieve the icing sugar, blend with the caster sugar and cornflour. Gradually whisk half the sugar mixture into the egg whites, then fold in the remainder of the sugar; lastly fold in the vinegar. Place the meringue in an icing bag fitted with a star pipe. Pipe round the pencil shape and over the entire centre. Pipe round the edge, building up to form a flan shape, or you can make a large flat surface. Bake in the coolest part of a very cool oven, 110°C, 225°F, Gas Mark ¼, for 3-4 hours until dry and crisp. Lift off the tray or paper while still warm. Cool and store in an airtight tin. Do not fill until just before required; this takes only a moment if the ingredients are ready, so whip the cream or have the ice cream at the correct consistency and prepare the fruit. Spoon the cream or ice cream into the case or over the meringue. Top with fruit then decorate with more cream or ice cream. See colour picture on page 93.

To freeze ahead
Meringues can be put into a freezer but, due to the high amount of sugar, they never freeze hard.

Note: The Pavlova can be baked more quickly if serving the same day; this produces a crisp outside, but a softer centre. Put in the oven at 150°C, 300°F, Gas Mark 2 for 5-10 minutes, reduce the heat to 140°C, 275°F, Gas Mark 1, for 1¼ hours.

Crème Caramel

Serves 6
For the caramel
150g (5oz) granulated or caster sugar
6tbspn water

For the custard
7 egg yolks or 2 whole eggs and 4 egg yolks
40-50g (1½-2oz) caster sugar
900ml (1½pt) milk or single cream or use half milk and half double cream

Variation
Crème Brûlée: Omit the caramel. Cook the custard; when cold top with a layer of flaked blanched almonds, then a thick coating of brown sugar, brown and crisp under the grill

Pavlova

Serves 6-8
4 egg whites
few drops vanilla essence
115g (4oz) icing sugar and 110g (4oz) caster sugar OR
225g (8oz) caster sugar
1tspn cornflour
1tspn white or brown malt vinegar

For the filling
150-300 ml (¼-½ pt) double cream or ice cream, fresh or canned fruit

Variations
1 Nut Pavlova: Add 50-75g (2-3oz) finely chopped walnuts to the meringue mixture with the vinegar
2 Small Meringues: Use the Pavlova recipe but omit the cornflour and vinegar. Pipe or spoon on to prepared tins. Bake for about 2 hours or until dry and crisp. It is possible to set meringues in the hot cupboard of a Hostess trolley: allow the same time as in an oven

Fruit Flan

Cream the sugar and butter or margarine until soft and light, add the flour, egg yolk and water to bind and knead well; chill if a little soft. Roll out and line a 20cm (8in) flan ring on an upturned baking tray. Put a piece of foil or greased greaseproof paper and crusts of bread on to the pastry. Bake the flan without a filling (known as 'baking blind') in the centre of a moderate to moderately hot oven, 190-200°C, 375-400°F, Gas Mark 5-6 for 20 minutes; remove the foil or greaseproof paper etc and flan ring after 15 minutes. Allow the flan to cool. Drain the fruit well; arrange in the flan. Blend the arrowroot and syrup, put into a saucepan. Add the sieved jam or jelly (the choice depends upon the colour of the fruit). Stir over a low heat, cook until thickened and clear. Cool slightly, spread over the fruit and leave to set. If using raw fruit or serving the flan hot (picture page 40) use a different glaze. For this, heat the sieved jam or jelly and water or syrup (see Variation on right). Put the hot fruit into the hot pastry, top with the hot glaze. Decorate with almonds. For raw fruit, allow the glaze to cool, then coat the fruit.

Short crust pastry could be used instead of fleur pastry. Sieve 225g (8oz) plain flour and a pinch salt; rub in 110g (4oz) butter or margarine. Bind with water, or an egg yolk and water.

Profiteroles

Put the water and butter into a good-sized saucepan, to allow room to beat the mixture. Bring the water to the boil. Remove the pan from the heat, add the flour and salt, beat well, then stir over a very low heat until the flour mixture forms a ball. Cool slightly. Whisk the eggs well, add gradually to the flour mixture and beat until smooth and glossy. Place in a piping bag with a 1cm (½in) plain nozzle. Pipe 18 small rounds, well spaced, on to a greased baking tray. Bake in the centre of a hot oven, 220°C, 425°F, Gas Mark 7, for 15-20 minutes. When cooked, slit the choux buns and leave to cool. Whip the cream and pipe or spoon into the profiteroles. Arrange in a pyramid shape on a cake stand or dish and spoon the chocolate sauce over the top. If preferred, the sauce can be kept hot and spooned over each portion. See colour picture opposite.

Chocolate Sauce

Break the chocolate into small pieces. Put the sugars, cocoa and vanilla essence into a saucepan. Blend the cornflour with a little milk until smooth; add to the sugar mixture together with the remaining milk. Stir over low heat until the sugars dissolve, then boil for 2 minutes. Remove from the heat, add the chocolate and butter and stir until melted and well blended. Serve hot or cold according to the recipe.

Fruit Flan

Serves 6
For the flan (fleur) pastry
40g (1½oz) caster sugar
95g (3½oz) butter or margarine
175g (6oz) flour, preferably plain
1 egg yolk
little water

For the filling
450g (1lb) cooked or canned fruit
1tspn arrowroot
150ml (¼pt) fruit syrup
2tbspn apricot jam or redcurrant jelly

Variation
With raw fruit, or if serving hot, you need 5tbspn jam or jelly and 2tbspn water or syrup

Profiteroles

Serves 6
For the choux pastry
150ml (¼pt) water
50g (2oz) butter
65g (2½oz) flour
pinch salt
2 eggs

For the filling
300ml (½pt) double cream

For the topping
Chocolate Sauce

Chocolate Sauce

Serves 6
50g (2oz) plain chocolate
100g (4oz) caster sugar
100g (4oz) soft brown sugar
75g (3oz) cocoa powder
1tspn vanilla essence
2tspn cornflour
300ml (½pt) milk
25g (1oz) butter

(opposite) Profiteroles with Chocolate Sauce

8 Take Pot-Luck

Much has been written in this book about the importance of thinking ahead to ensure super entertaining. It certainly is true that careful pre-planning is advisable, but there will be occasions when you have no time to do any planning and must improvise extra courses or create more interesting dishes. The suggestions below will, I hope, be helpful.

If there are no ingredients in the house to make a soup, then make a thin White Sauce (use twice as much milk as the recipe on page 79). Add about 175g (6oz) diced cheese — most cheeses are suitable, but blue-veined cheeses such as Stilton or Danish Blue are super. Heat in the sauce with a little cream, then serve.

Fish-Stuffed Pancakes

Serves 10-12
pancakes as page 103, but use double quantity
cheese sauce as page 79, but use treble quantity
1.5kg (3lb) cooked white or shell fish or use a mixture of fish

To garnish
lemon
parsley

Fish-Stuffed Pancakes

Prepare and cook the pancakes; allow one large or two smaller pancakes per person. Make the sauce. Use just one-third of this to blend with the fish. Fill the pancakes with the fish and sauce mixture. Spoon a little sauce into one or two oven-proof dishes. Place the pancakes on top of this. Add the rest of the sauce. This can be done ahead. Cover the dishes tightly and heat the pancakes for approximately 30 minutes in the centre of a moderately hot oven, 200°C, 400°F, Gas Mark 6.

To keep the food hot
Place in the hot cupboard of the Hostess trolley or cabinet, on a heat tray or in a cool oven.

To freeze ahead
These filled pancakes freeze well for up to 3 months.

Eggs in Brown Butter

Serves 8
4 large thin slices bread
100g (4oz) butter
2tspn Worcestershire sauce
1tspn lemon juice or white wine vinegar
shake cayenne pepper
1tbspn chopped parsley
8 eggs

Eggs in Brown Butter

Cut the bread into 8 croûtons, sufficiently large to support the eggs. Heat half the butter in a large frying pan and fry the croûtons until crisp and brown. Put on to a hot serving dish and keep hot while cooking the eggs. Heat the remaining butter in the frying pan until it turns dark brown, add the rest of the ingredients except the eggs; heat thoroughly, then break the eggs into the browned butter, fry these until set, basting once or twice with the butter. Lift the eggs on to the croûtons, spoon the brown butter over the top and serve at once.

To freeze ahead
It is useful to store fried croûtons in the freezer.

Shrimps in Brown Butter

Prepare the croûtons and browned butter as the recipe above, add the well-dried shrimps and capers. Heat for 2 minutes only. Spoon on to the croûtons and serve.

For a more substantial dish, combine the eggs and shrimps, but keep the proportions of butter etc the same.

Gaiety Salad

Cook the pasta shapes in boiling salted water as directed on the packet, drain, rinse in cold water, then drain again well. Hard-boil the eggs, gently crack the shells, plunge the eggs into cold water (this prevents the possibility of a dark line forming round the yolks), cool, then shell and quarter. Cook the vegetables as directed on the packet, drain and allow to cool. Drain and flake the tuna fish; dice the onions, skin and quarter the tomatoes. Mix the mayonnaise, soured cream or yoghurt and mustard together in a fairly large bowl. Carefully fold in the pasta shapes, eggs, mixed vegetables, tuna, onions and tomatoes. Shred the Chinese leaves or lettuce, put on a dish or into a salad bowl (Chinese leaves give a new flavour and are exceptionally crisp and appetising). Pile the salad mixture on to the Chinese leaves or lettuce, garnish with the watercress, olives and slices or wedges of lemon.

Scalloped Salmon

Drain the salmon, measure the liquid and add enough milk to give 450ml (¾pt). Flake the fish; grate the cheese. Butter four natural scallop shells or four individual oven-proof dishes. Coat the insides with some fine breadcrumbs and spoon in the salmon flakes, pile these higher in the centre. Melt the butter, stir in the flour and cook for 2-3 minutes. Remove the pan from the heat and gradually stir in the milk and liquid from the salmon can. Bring to the boil and continue to stir until it thickens. Add 50g (2oz) of the cheese, salt and pepper to taste. Spoon the sauce over the salmon scallops. Sprinkle with the remaining breadcrumbs and cheese and brown under the grill for a few minutes. See colour picture on page 65.

To keep the food hot
Do not cover, put into the hot cupboard of the Hostess trolley or cabinet, or on to a heat tray or in a cool oven.

To freeze ahead
Prepare the dishes and freeze. Reheat in a low oven from the frozen state. Use within a month.

Shrimps in Brown Butter

Serves 8
Ingredients as opposite, but
   use 450g (1lb) peeled shrimps
   instead of the eggs with
   1tbspn capers

Gaiety Salad

Serves 4
175g (6oz) pasta shapes
salt to taste
3 eggs
1 small packet mixed frozen
   vegetables
1 198g (7oz) can tuna fish
4 spring onions
4 tomatoes
4tbspn mayonnaise
4tbspn soured cream or yoghurt
1tspn made mustard
Chinese leaves or lettuce

To garnish
small bunch watercress
50g (2oz) black olives
1 lemon

Scalloped Salmon

Serves 4
213g (7½oz) can pink or red
   salmon
450ml (¾pt) milk and salmon
   liquid
75g (3oz) Cheddar cheese
50g (2oz) soft breadcrumbs
40g (1½oz) butter
40g (1½oz) flour
salt and pepper

111

9 One-Dish Parties

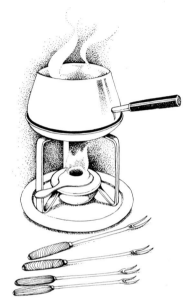

Fondue pan for meat fondues

Meat Fondue

Serves 8
1.5kg (3lb) good quality lean
    lamb (leg preferably) or
    rump or fillet steak or use
    tender chicken

For the marinade
1 garlic clove
1tbspn Worcestershire sauce
2tbspn red wine
salt and pepper

For frying
oil

To serve
dips as given below

Easy dips
Blend Mayonnaise or
Hollandaise Sauce (recipes
pages 64 and 79) with curry
powder; with tomato purée;
with 1tspn capers and 1-2tspn
chopped fresh herbs

Do not imagine you have to prepare an elaborate meal when you entertain; you can invite people to join you for a glass of wine or just a cup of tea or coffee, offer a sandwich or plate of biscuits and still create the warmth of atmosphere and genuine welcome that is an essential part of good entertaining.

Food does, however, play an important part in most entertaining and the suggestions on this and the following pages assume you are entertaining in the easy way with just one main dish. Consider some of the dishes you could provide:

Sausages and Mash, served with beer or cider.
A Pâté Party; one or more kinds of pâté, with salad and crisp rolls or crispbread, served with wine (see pages 67 and 68).
A Cheese and Wine Party, see page 116.
Dishes based on pasta and rice (see the next two pages) served with white, red or rosé wine.
A Salad Party (ideal for slimmers); one or more salads, served with white wine or fruit juice.
To be more ambitious have:
An Hors d'Oeuvre Party, with a selection of hot and cold dishes, see pages 59 to 66.

Meat Fondue

Remember the oil is very hot, so use a metal fondue pan and read the advice on safety, page 17. You can heat the oil on the cooker in the kitchen and then bring it into the dining room and stand it over the table heater.

Cut the meat into cubes — do not make these too large, otherwise the heat cannot penetrate sufficiently quickly to cook the meat well. Peel and crush the garlic, blend with the sauce and wine, plus salt and pepper to taste. Pour into a large shallow dish. Add the meat and marinate for 3-4 hours.

Pour the oil into the fondue pan; do not have more than two-thirds full. Arrange the meat in an attractive container, with the various dips around. Heat the oil sufficiently for the meat to cook within a few minutes. Each person spears a cube of meat on a fondue fork, places it into the hot oil until cooked, then removes it, replaces the fondue fork with an ordinary fork and dips the meat into the accompaniments.

To freeze ahead
While defrosted frozen lamb can be used, I find it is a little less firm than fresh lamb, so prefer not to use it. Defrosted beef or chicken can be used.

112

(opposite) Smoked Mackerel Risotto

Cooking Rice

Long grain rice is a perfect accompaniment to many dishes.

To each 25g (1oz) ordinary long grain rice you need 60ml (2 fl oz) water and salt to taste. Put the rice, cold water and salt into a pan. Bring to the boil, stir with a fork, cover the pan, lower the heat. Simmer for 15 minutes, or until the rice is tender and the liquid absorbed. Fluff up with a fork. If using par-boiled long grain rice, allow 75ml (2½fl oz) water to each 25g (1oz) rice, simmer for 20 minutes. If using Italian (medium grain) rice, allow 90ml (3 fl oz) water to each 25g (1oz) rice, simmer for 25 minutes. In such recipes as the Risotto or Paella, more liquid is needed as the mixture should be pleasantly moist. If using brown rice, allow 120ml (4 fl oz) water to each 25g (1oz) brown rice. Cook for 35 minutes, or as on packet.

To freeze ahead
Cooked rice freezes well for 3 months. Freeze lightly, fork the rice, continuing freezing.

Paella

Serves 4
1 small frying chicken
1 small onion
1 garlic clove
3tbspn oil
900ml (1½pt) chicken stock or
    water and 2 chicken stock
    cubes
2 medium tomatoes
1 red pepper
225g (8oz) long grain rice
large pinch saffron
12 large peeled prawns
12 cooked or bottled mussels
small packet frozen peas
salt and pepper
2-3tbspn Spanish stuffed olives

Mackerel Risotto

Serves 4
Peel and thinly slice a small onion, wipe and quarter 100-175g (4-6oz) mushrooms; slice a large green pepper, discard the core and seeds; skin and chop 3-4 large tomatoes.

The recipe illustrated opposite was made with smoked mackerel; fresh mackerel could be used, but add salt when cooking the fish. Place 450g (1lb) smoked mackerel in a little water in a good-sized pan, simmer for 6-8 minutes, drain and flake. Heat 50g (2oz) butter in the same pan, add the onion and cook for several minutes, then put in 225g (8oz) long grain or Italian rice (see left) together with 750-900ml (1¼-1½pt) chicken or fish stock. Cover the pan, simmer for 10 minutes, then add the mushrooms and pepper. Continue cooking, stirring once or twice, for 10-20 minutes (depending upon the kind of rice used) or until the rice is tender and the excess liquid absorbed. Stir in the tomatoes, mackerel, another 25g (1oz) butter, salt and pepper to taste. Cook gently for a few minutes. See colour picture on page 113.

To keep the food hot
Spoon into heated Hostess trolley dishes or into a casserole with a tightly fitting lid and place on a heat tray or in a cool oven.

To freeze ahead
Freeze lightly, fork to separate the ingredients, continue freezing. Use within 6 weeks.

Paella

The word Paella indicates that the food can be cooked and served in the same dish, but you can cook the ingredients in an ordinary frying pan and keep them hot as above. Joint the chicken; the bones can be removed if desired. Peel and chop the onion and garlic. Heat the oil in a large container; fry the onion and garlic with the chicken until golden. Add half the stock or water and 1 stock cube and simmer for 15 minutes. Skin and dice the tomatoes, cut the pepper into neat pieces, add to the onion together with the rice and remaining stock or water and stock cube. Simmer for 5 minutes, stirring once or twice. Stir in the saffron. If planning to cook and serve in the same dish arrange the prawns and mussels attractively and add the peas, salt and pepper to taste and the olives. Continue cooking for a further 10 minutes or until the rice has absorbed most of the liquid and the additional ingredients are really hot. See colour picture on page 121.

To freeze ahead
This dish is better eaten when freshly made, but defrosted chicken and prawns could be used.

To keep rice hot
Add 1tbspn of olive or good quality oil to the water in which rice is cooked. Cover cooked rice well to prevent drying. A heated Hostess trolley or cabinet dish is ideal.

114

Polynesian Beef

Cut the beef into narrow strips about 5-8cm (2-3in) in length and 1.5cm (¾in) wide and thick. Peel the onions and chop finely. Cut the pulp of the peppers into small dice; discard the cores and seeds. Chop the celery; drain and chop the water chestnuts. Heat the oil in a strong saucepan or deep frying pan and cook the meat with the onions for 5 minutes, stir once or twice. Add the other vegetables and cook for 2-3 minutes only. Blend the cornflour with the soy sauce and stock, or water and stock cube, pour into the pan, stir as the mixture thickens; add salt and pepper to taste. Cover the pan, lower the heat and simmer steadily for 15 minutes only. Add the bean shoots for the last 2-3 minutes only. While the meat mixture is cooking, boil the rice; serve the beef mixture with the cooked rice.

To keep the food hot
Cook all ingredients lightly to retain their texture. Cover the serving dish and put on a heat tray, into a cool oven, or use a covered Hostess trolley or cabinet dish. Serve as soon as possible.

To freeze ahead
Take care not to over-cook if freezing, so the vegetables retain texture; use within 3 months.

Spaghetti Bolognese

Wash, dry and finely chop the mushrooms; do not skin these if good quality as the skins give extra flavour. Peel and finely chop the onions; shred, grate or finely dice the carrots; peel and crush the garlic. A little garlic salt could be substituted when seasoning the sauce. Heat the butter and oil together in a saucepan; the oil gives extra flavour and prevents the butter over-heating. Add the vegetables and fry for just a few seconds. Stir in the minced meat, fry until crumbly; this takes 2-3 minutes. Add all the other ingredients, except the spaghetti and cheese, stir continuously as the sauce comes to the boil. Cover the pan, simmer for 30 minutes or until the meat is tender and the sauce becomes thick and rich; if necessary, lift the lid towards the end of the cooking time so any extra liquid evaporates; remove the bay leaves. Meanwhile cook the spaghetti as directed on the packet and drain well, pile on to a hot dish. To serve, top the spaghetti with the sauce and a sprinkling of the cheese, serve extra cheese separately.

To keep the food hot
Rinse the spaghetti after cooking in boiling water; this prevents it becoming sticky with storage. Return to the pan with a knob of butter or a little oil, reheat. The covered dishes in a Hostess trolley or cabinet are ideal for keeping both the spaghetti and the meat sauce hot. I would put them separately, or you can use other covered dishes and keep the food hot in a low oven or on a heat tray.

To freeze ahead
The sauce freezes well for up to 3 months.

Polynesian Beef

Serves 4
550g (1¼lb) topside of beef
2 medium onions
1 green pepper
1 red pepper
few sticks of celery
2-3 canned water chestnuts
2tbspn oil
1tbspn cornflour
1tbspn soy sauce
300ml (½pt) beef stock or water and 1 beef stock cube
salt and pepper
100g (4oz) fresh or canned bean shoots

To serve
225g (8oz) long grain rice

Variation
When water chestnuts are not available, use lightly cooked turnips or cooked chestnuts

Spaghetti Bolognese

Serves 6-8 as a main dish or 8-12 as an hors d'oeuvre

For the sauce
100g (4oz) mushrooms
2 medium onions
2 medium carrots
2-3 garlic cloves (optional)
50g (2oz) butter
2tbspn olive oil
450g (1lb) raw minced steak or beef
8tbspn tomato purée (or use small can or tube)
2 bay leaves
600ml (1pt) beef stock or water and 2 beef stock cubes
2 wineglasses red wine or use extra stock
salt and pepper

450g (1lb) spaghetti

To serve
grated Parmesan cheese

115

Selection of Cheeses

Group 1: Familiar Cheeses
Many people are conservative about cheese so have Cheddar, Cheshire, Edam, Gouda, Gruyère, Lancashire, Port Salut, Wensleydale.

Group 2: Familiar but Creamy
Boursin, Brie, Camembert, Pont l'Evèque. Check that Brie and Camembert are soft and ripe but NOT over-ripe.

Group 3: Veined Cheeses
Danish Blue, Gorgonzola, Roquefort, Stilton.

Group 4: Lesser-known Cheeses
Dolcelatte (blue-veined but creamy), Esrom (mild Danish cheese), Limburger (strong cheese), Livarot (a refreshing cheese), Romano (Italian cream cheese), Sage Derby (includes sage leaves), Tomme de Marc de Raisin (grape-skinned coated cheese).

Amounts to allow per person
At least 50g (2oz) for a cheese course at the end of a meal or 175-225g (6-8oz) for a Cheese and Wine Party.

Wines to serve at a Cheese and Wine Party

(See note on page 35)

White Wines
See page 29; consider also inexpensive Val de Loire, Bulgarian Pinot Chardonnay, Soave. Sweeter Sauternes blends well with a 'biting' cheese like Gorgonzola.

Red Wines
See page 31; consider also inexpensive Bourgogne Rouge Champrenard, Le Piat de Beaujolais, Côte du Rhône, Langunilla Rioja Tinto, Chianti.

About Cheese

The cheese board should look as colourful as the other dishes in a meal, so garnish it with fruit, radishes, celery, etc. The cheeses have been put into groups; and it would be interesting to choose a cheese from each group. Do not, however, feel you must have a selection of cheeses; a whole perfect Brie would be a good choice at the end of the meal. ALWAYS allow cheese to stand at room temperature for at least one hour before serving.

Cheese Soufflé

Serves 6 as a savoury at the end of a meal
This can be served as a light main course or a savoury at the end of a meal. While the soufflé must be served as soon as it is cooked, the prepared uncooked mixture can be placed into the soufflé dish, completely covered with an upturned bowl (to exclude the air) and left standing for up to an hour before baking.

Butter the inside of an 18cm (7in) soufflé dish; if a shallow dish is used, tie a deep band of greased greaseproof paper round the top to support the mixture as it rises.

Heat 40g (1½oz) butter in a large saucepan, add 40g (1½oz) flour, stir over a low heat for 2-3 minutes. Blend in 275ml (scant ½pt) milk and stir over the heat until a thick sauce. Add 3tbspn double cream. Separate the yolks from the whites of 5 eggs, whisk the yolks into the sauce with 175g (6oz) grated Gruyère or Cheddar cheese, salt, pepper, and a little made mustard. Whisk the egg whites until stiff and fold into the cheese mixture then spoon into the soufflé dish. Bake in the centre of a moderate oven, 190°C, 375°F, Gas Mark 5 for 30-35 minutes until well risen and golden brown. This soufflé should be slightly soft in the centre.

Cheese Fondue

Serves 4
The recipe below is for a classic fondue, but other good cooking cheeses, such as Cheddar, could be used. If you do not possess a fondue pan and heater, use a strong saucepan placed over a very low heat. When the cheese *starts to melt* spoon the mixture into a heated Hostess trolley or cabinet dish. DO NOT keep a fondue hot on a heat tray or in an oven as this could spoil the smooth texture.

Grate 225g (8oz) Gruyère and 225g (8oz) Emmenthal cheese. Rub the inside of the fondue pan with a little butter and a cut clove of garlic (this is optional). Add the cheeses to the pan. Blend 1tspn cornflour with 300ml (½pt) dry white wine, add to the pan, together with a very little salt, but a good shake of pepper, 1-2tbspn Kirsch or brandy could be added.

Place the pan over the fondue heater, stir from time to time until the cheese melts, then reduce the heat. Prepare squares of fresh bread or toast. Everyone spears these on fondue forks and dips them into the hot cheese mixture.

10 Come to Tea or Coffee

It is traditional to serve tiny sandwiches with afternoon tea, together with scones, some kind of cake or gâteau and home-made biscuits. These are equally good with coffee.

The picture below and recipes on page 118 give unusual ideas for serving sandwiches. There is a recipe for a special Celebration cake on page 120 and gâteaux on page 100.

Good tea, like good coffee, depends upon buying a first-class brand and making the beverage correctly. Use freshly drawn water from the cold tap, bring this to the boil and make the tea immediately the water reaches boiling point. Always warm the pot before making the tea. You could offer your guests a choice of Indian or China tea. It is usual to serve China tea with lemon, rather than milk; some people prefer lemon to milk with Indian tea. Cut thin slices of lemon, remove the pips, and have these available.

Amount of Tea

The old adage is to allow one teaspoon of tea per person and 'one for the pot'. This is completely satisfactory for most people.

If making tea for a large number of people you need to allow approximately 40g (1½oz) tea for each 4.5L (8pt) water or you could use the equivalent in tea bags.

Sandwich Kebabs and Party Roll-Ups

To Keep Sandwiches Fresh
Cover with clingfilm or foil or slightly damp kitchen paper until ready to serve.

To freeze ahead
Place the Roll-Ups in a shallow foil or polythene container. Seal and freeze. To freeze the Sandwich Kebabs, wrap the whole sandwiches in freezer film or foil, seal and freeze. Cut into squares while still slightly frozen. Use within 2 months.

More Scones
Fruit Scones: Add 50-75g (2-3oz) dried fruit.

Treacle Scones: Omit the sugar and add 2tbspn black treacle before adding the milk.

Cheese Scones: Season the flour, omit the sugar; add 75g (3oz) grated cheese.

More Biscuits
Chocolate Shortbreads: Omit 25g (1oz) flour and add 25g (1oz) cocoa powder. Top the biscuits with melted chocolate when cold.

Coconut Shortbreads: Work 50g (2oz) desiccated coconut into the mixture before rolling into balls.

Interesting Sandwiches
The picture on page 117 shows that sandwiches can look both original and interesting.
To make the Sandwich Kebabs:
a) Blend approximately 225g (8oz) minced lean ham, 1tbspn Worcestershire sauce and 75g (3oz) butter; sandwich 24 large slices of white bread with this mixture.
b) Blend 100g (4oz) butter, 225g (8oz) grated Cheddar cheese and ½tspn made mustard; sandwich 24 large slices brown bread with this mixture.
Cut each sandwich into 16 squares, put on cocktail sticks, as shown in the picture, press into a grapefruit or large, foil-covered potato. Garnish with radish roses and parsley.

To make the Party Roll-Ups:
a) Chop finely 100g (4oz) mushrooms and cook in 25g (1oz) butter until soft. Blend with 225g (8oz) liver pâté and a little salt and pepper. Remove the crusts from 12 large slices of white bread, spread with the pâté and mushroom mixture.
b) Blend 225g (8oz) cream cheese, 2 tbspn tomato purée and a little salt and pepper. Remove the crusts from 12 large slices of brown bread and spread with this mixture. Roll the slices of bread like a Swiss roll, trim the ends if necessary, and arrange on a plate.

Scones
Sieve 225g (8oz) self-raising flour, or plain flour and 2tspn baking powder, and a pinch of salt. Rub in 25-50g (1-2oz) butter or margarine, add 25-50g (1-2oz) sugar. Mix with enough milk to make a soft rolling consistency. Roll out to 2.5cm (1in) in thickness, cut into about 15-20 tiny rounds. Place on a baking tray and cook for 10 minutes towards the top of a hot oven, 220°C, 425°F, Gas Mark 7. Serve hot or cold. Split and butter, or serve topped with whipped cream and jam.

Shortbread Crisps
Cream together 175g (6oz) butter or margarine and 110g (4oz) caster sugar. Sieve 225g (8oz) self-raising flour, or plain flour and 2 level tspn baking powder, into the mixture. Knead and form into about 36 small balls. Place on ungreased baking trays, allowing plenty of room to spread, and bake in the centre of a very moderate oven, 160°C, 325°F, Gas Mark 3 for 12 minutes, cool on the trays.

These biscuits can be decorated with glacé cherries before baking, or iced when cooked and cooled.

Brandy Snaps

It is important to have very slightly less flour than the other ingredients. If weighing with metric scales the measurements given ensure this, but if weighing with Imperial scales then take away 1tspn flour. Sieve the flour and ginger. Put the butter, sugar and golden syrup into a saucepan, heat only until the butter and sugar have dissolved, then add the flour mixture. Grease 2 or 3 flat baking trays, or use 'non-stick' trays; do not flour these. Put teaspoons of the mixture on to the trays, allowing plenty of room for the mixture to spread in cooking. It is a good idea to put only one tray in the oven at the beginning of the cooking period so you roll these biscuits before the next tray is ready. Bake the biscuits in the centre of a very moderate oven, 160°C, 325°F, Gas Mark 3 for 8-10 minutes, or until uniformly golden brown. You can put the second tray into the oven after about 5 minutes and the third tray in when removing the first (all trays must be as near the centre of the oven as possible). Allow the cooked biscuits to cool for about 2 minutes, or until they can be lifted off the baking tray quite easily. Remove with a palette knife and roll round the greased handles of wooden spoons; hold in position for a few seconds to set, then slip off the spoon handles and place on to a wire cooling tray. When quite cool, store in an airtight tin, away from all other biscuits.

Dutch Ginger Shortcake

Line a Swiss roll tin measuring approximately 32 x 23cm (13 x 9in) with greased greaseproof paper. Drain the ginger, chop finely, retain the syrup. Dry the almonds well if you have blanched and split these yourself, although one can buy packs of ready-blanched almonds. Sieve the flour, or flour and baking powder, into a mixing bowl. Rub in the butter until the mixture looks like fine breadcrumbs. Add the sugar, egg and ginger syrup. Stir the mixture well to blend. Spoon into the lined tin and spread flat with a floured knife or spoon. Press the ginger and almonds firmly into the cake mixture.

Bake in the centre of a moderate oven, 180°C, 350°F, Gas Mark 4 for 30-35 minutes until lightly browned. Reduce the heat slightly after 20 minutes if necessary. Cool slightly, then mark in fingers while still in the tin. When cold, remove from the tin. This shortcake keeps well for some weeks in an airtight container, away from other biscuits, cakes, bread or pastry.

See colour picture on page 101.

Brandy Snaps

Makes 18
50g (2oz) flour, preferably plain (see method)
½tspn ground ginger
55g (2oz) butter
55g (2oz) caster or demerara sugar
2 level tbspn golden syrup

Variations
1 Honey Snaps: Use thin honey in place of golden syrup
2 Brandy Cones: Roll the mixture round greased cream horn tins instead of spoon handles
3 Parisienne Biscuits: Bake the biscuits for 4-5 minutes until the mixture has spread out, then top with a sprinkling of finely chopped blanched almonds and crystallised peel. Continue baking; do not roll

Dutch Ginger Shortcake

Makes 20-24 fingers
210g (7½oz) jar stem (preserved) ginger in syrup
100g (4oz) blanched split almonds
450g (1lb) self-raising flour, or plain flour with 4 level tspn baking powder
225g (8oz) unsalted butter
225g (8oz) light Muscovado sugar
1 egg

Baking Rich Cakes

Baking times may vary according to your particular oven

The way to check
After one-third of the *total* baking time, the cake should hardly have changed colour and be very soft; if darkening lower the heat. After about two-thirds of the total baking time, it should be golden-brown but still be fairly soft; if darkening too much, lay thick paper over the top of the tin and lower the heat slightly.
To test after baking, first press firmly on top — the cake should feel firm; if it has shrunk away from the sides of the tin, remove from the oven and listen. If it gives a definite faint humming noise it is not quite cooked, so return to the oven. Cool in the tin, turn out carefully; wrap in foil, store in an airtight tin.

To Ice the Cake

Brush away any crumbs from the cake, coat with a little sieved apricot jam.
Roll out the marzipan to a size to cover the cake, press against this to give a smooth coating. Roll lightly. If you have worked quickly you could put on the icing at once; if not, leave the cake for 48 hours for the marzipan to dry out.
Spread the Royal icing over the cake, leave to become completely hard, then use any icing left to pipe a design around the base and on top.

Celebration Cake

To make a 23cm (9in) round cake, line the base of the tin with a double round of brown paper and a double thickness of lightly greased greaseproof paper. Line the sides of the tin with greased greaseproof paper. Tie a double band of brown paper round the tin; this keeps the cake moist and protects it during baking.

Sieve together 350g (12oz) plain flour, 1tspn each of ground cinnamon and allspice and a pinch of salt. Chop 110g (4oz) candied peel, 110g (4oz) glacé cherries and 50-110g (2-4oz) blanched almonds. Mix with 900g (2lb) mixed dried fruit.

Finely grate the rind from 1 lemon and 1 orange, cream with 225g (8oz) butter or best margarine, 225g (8oz) sugar (preferably dark moist brown) and 1tbspn black treacle, until soft. Blend 4 large eggs with 4tbspn sherry, brandy or rum, gradually add to the creamed mixture, together with the sieved dry ingredients. Lastly, stir in the fruit mixture. Put the cake mixture into the tin, smooth quite flat on top. Press with damp, but not over-wet, knuckles. Bake in the centre of a very moderate oven, 160°C, 325°F, Gas Mark 3. Cook at this temperature for 1½ hours, then lower the temperature to 140-150°C, 275-300°F, Gas Mark 1-2 for a further 1½-2 hours, or until cooked (see left).

This cake should be made at least a month before being required, and stored in an airtight tin. To give a very moist texture, prick at weekly intervals with a metal skewer and spoon a little sweet sherry or brandy or rum over the cake.

Marzipan

Sieve 175g (6oz) icing sugar, then blend with 350g (12oz) ground almonds, 175g (6oz) caster sugar and a few drops almond essence. Bind with the yolks of 3 eggs. This should give sufficient moisture to gather the marzipan mixture together. Put the marzipan on to a sugared board, roll out and coat the cake (see left).

Royal Icing

Sieve 900g (2lb) icing sugar very carefully. Whisk the whites of 4 eggs lightly by hand or with a mixer; do not over-beat as this produces air bubbles which make it difficult to achieve a smooth coating and prevents the icing flowing smoothly through the icing pipe for piping. Add the icing sugar, 1-2tbspn lemon juice and 2-3tspn glycerine (this is not essential, but helps to produce a slightly less hard icing). Beat the mixture only until white and shining. Put any icing required for piping in a separate bowl, cover with a damp cloth. This quantity gives one coating and a limited amount of piping.

(opposite) Paella ready to serve in the Hostess Hotpot heat tray (see page 114)

Quantity of Coffee

Use approximately 4 level tbspn ground coffee to 600 ml (1pt) water, or
225-275g (8-10oz) ground coffee to 4.5L (8pt) water.

Note: A small 'after-dinner' coffee cup holds approximately 90ml (3 fl oz), so you obtain 6-7 cups from 600ml (1pt) coffee. The average teacup holds approximately 150ml (5 fl oz), so you would obtain 4 cups from 600ml (1pt) coffee, if drunk 'black'. If serving 'half coffee' and 'half milk' you obtain 6-8 cups.
Use approximately 4 level tspn instant coffee to 600ml (1pt) water, or
50-70g (2-2½oz) instant coffee to 4.5L (8pt) water.

Note: If the coffee, or instant coffee, contains chicory, as French brands of coffee often do, then you could be a little sparing in measuring the quantities above. It is always better to err on the side of making strong coffee, which can be diluted to personal taste with boiling water or with milk. You can buy after-dinner brands of coffee; the coffee beans have been lightly roasted to give an ideal coffee for drinking without cream or milk, or with the minimum of cream or milk.

Glacé Icing

This is softer icing than Royal icing, and is therefore ideal for soft sponge cakes or petits fours.
Sieve icing sugar into a basin, blend with enough water, orange or lemon juice or liquid coffee to give a coating consistency.
To coat tiny squares of sponge with the icing insert a fine skewer into the cake. Dip into the icing, so that the top and sides are coated.

Perfect Coffee

Take a pride in producing a perfect cup of coffee at the end of a good meal, or for coffee parties (see also page 122).

Buy coffee ground freshly, or choose the vacuum-packed type; coffee deteriorates rapidly unless kept in a tightly-sealed container. If you buy coffee in a paper bag, keep away from strongly-smelling foods in the shopping basket; transfer to a screw-topped jar.

Use freshly drawn water from the cold tap; do not use the hot tap, and make the coffee as soon as the water comes to the boil. Use the correct amount of coffee (see left).

Appreciate the different methods of roasting coffee; an American roast gives a mild, light-coloured coffee; a French roast, darker stronger coffee. Choose a finely ground coffee if you use a jug or saucepan, but medium ground for a percolator, Cona or drip-type of coffee maker. Fine coffee forms a solid 'mat', through which the water cannot flow easily. It is ideal to buy coffee beans and grind these before use. You must have a proper coffee grinder; do not use a liquidiser.

Never serve boiled or boiling milk with coffee; this changes the flavour of the drink. Ideally one should add cold milk or cream, or the special product made for coffee. If you like hot milk, bring this to simmering point only. Select single, rather than double, cream (except for Irish coffee). Hold the coffee spoon over the coffee, with the bowl side downwards. Pour the cream slowly over the spoon into the coffee to prevent curdling.

To keep coffee hot
Specialist coffee-makers, such as percolators, are generally thermostatically controlled, so keep the coffee hot. If you have a utensil with a flat base, you could keep the coffee hot for a limited period on a heat tray. If you have to prepare a large amount of coffee without specialist equipment, strain each batch of coffee (as soon as made and infused) into a saucepan; cover tightly. Heat when required.

Petits Fours

These small 'nibbles' to serve with coffee are easily produced. Coat 'bite-sized' pieces of sponge (recipe page 100) with glacé icing or sieved apricot jam or whipped cream, then roll in chopped nuts or desiccated coconut. Ratafias (recipe page 106) look colourful if topped with pieces of glacé cherry before baking.

Use left-over marzipan (page 120) to fill stoned dessert dates, or tint it and mould into miniature fruits. Work a little peppermint essence and extra icing sugar into Royal icing (also on page 120), roll out, cut into rounds and leave to harden. These Peppermint Creams could then be coated in melted plain chocolate.

Methods of Making Coffee

In a jug
Heat the jug before making the coffee. Put in the correct quantity of coffee. Pour boiling water over the coffee; stir, then cover the jug. Leave in a warm place to infuse for 4 minutes, then strain into another heated jug.

In a saucepan
Bring the water to boiling point, add the correct quantity of coffee; stir briskly and allow to reach boiling point once more, stir again. Cover the saucepan with a lid, a plate or a folded cloth and leave in a warm place to infuse for 4 minutes, then strain into a heated jug.

Both the jug and saucepan methods produce excellent coffee. If entertaining visitors from Scandinavia, who tend to have a coffee-kettle boiling steadily, I would allow the coffee in the saucepan to simmer steadily for several minutes, before stirring and leaving to infuse.

In a percolator
Follow the specific instructions given by the manufacturer, but basically put the correct amount of coffee into the basket, add the cold water, then place the percolator over the heat or switch on the electricity. If the percolator is thermostatically controlled, it will keep the coffee simmering and/or keeping hot until required. If, however, the percolator is not automatic, check that the heat is turned very low as the coffee is left simmering.

In a Cona
Always check that the outside of the glass bowl is dry before putting over the heat. Put the cold water into the bottom bowl, fix the top bowl and filter-stem. Add the coffee, place over a low to medium heat, allow the water to rise into the top bowl; stir (being careful you do not dislodge the centre stem), then allow the filtered coffee to drop back into the bottom bowl. Keep warm over a low heat. You may prefer to allow the water in the bottom bowl to rise twice to give stronger coffee.

Drip (filter) method
These appliances vary appreciably and you must follow the specific instructions given by the manufacturer. Modern appliances generally have the means of keeping the coffee warm, as it stands, but if you need to place the filter and coffee over a jug, then pour on the boiling water, it is advisable to stand the jug on a heat tray, so the coffee keeps hot.

Note: If you do not have any means of keeping the prepared coffee hot, it may be worthwhile making this ahead of the party, straining then covering this, and reheating as required; or you could stand the jug of coffee in a pan of boiling water.

Irish Coffee
To make this beverage you need Irish Whiskey. If you have only Scotch Whisky, then you can call the drink 'Gaelic Coffee'. Pour a measure of whiskey into each warmed brandy glass, fill up with hot coffee (leave space for the cream). Pour enough double cream over an upturned spoon to give a thick layer on top of the coffee. You drink the hot strong coffee through the layer of rich cream. If guests like sweetened coffee, it is wiser for them to spoon the sugar into the hot coffee before adding the cream.

Iced Coffee
This is a delicious drink in hot weather or for a luncheon party. You must make very strong coffee; good instant coffee is excellent for iced coffee. If using ground coffee, strain, then chill.
There are various ways of serving Iced Coffee:
1 Put crushed ice into tumblers, top with the coffee, then add a spoonful of whipped cream.
2 Half-fill tumblers with ice-cold coffee, then fill up with ice-cold milk. Always keep the ingredients, ie coffee, milk, cream, in the refrigerator until ready to serve the coffee.
A very practical way of preparing Iced Coffee is to make double-strength coffee, then strain and allow to cool. Pour this into ice-making trays with the sections in place. Freeze the coffee. You then put one or more coffee-flavoured ice cubes in each tumbler and fill up with cold milk.

11 Clearing Up

The party is over — it has been a successful occasion and everyone has enjoyed themselves. No doubt you, the hostess, think longingly of relaxing or probably departing for bed, if the hour is late. It is, however, worthwhile spending a short time doing a little clearing-up, unless you have someone to do this for you.

First of all, empty any ashtrays if your guests were smokers. Few things are more unpleasant than to come into a room next morning which smells of stale tobacco. As you throw away the stubs of the cigars or cigarettes, make quite sure that none are smouldering. If there is time to leave windows open for a short while, do so. It is surprising how quickly the room becomes 'normal' again with a little good fresh air.

Gather up the glasses which will probably have the dregs of liqueur, wine or other drink in them; it is surprising how this gives an unpleasant smell to the room by the morning. Empty out the tiny amount of alcohol in the glasses and give these a quick rinse — if you have the energy. The glasses will not be sparklingly clean, but will be much easier to wash-up, especially if they have contained a liqueur, whose high sugar content makes the glasses very sticky if left unwashed for some hours. If you have time to wash glasses properly in hot water, then it is very rewarding to see them clean and sparkling again.

The kitchen or dining room may look depressingly full of dirty plates and cutlery. You may be the kind of person who likes to clear-up completely — if this is the case, you will go to work on them. There should be few, if any, dirty pots and pans if you have followed the advice on dishing-up ahead given on pages 42 to 47.

Even if you have no intention of doing all the washing-up until next day, there are certain sensible and speedy things you can do. Fill one or more strong jugs with hot detergent solution and stand the cutlery in these. Take care that the ivory handles of knives do not become wet as this spoils the colour and tends, over a period of time, to loosen the handles. Throw away any particles of food left on the plates; you could put the plates and serving dishes to soak in detergent solution or, if you have a dish-washer, fill that with the china and silverware.

Take a last look into the dining and sitting rooms. Shake up the cushions, so creases drop out. If anything has been spilled on the furniture or carpet, deal with this as the advice on pages 17 and 18. Check that any candles are extinguished, that fires are turned off in the case of electric or gas, or damped-down in the case of an open fire. Check that all electrical equipment, including the Hostess, is switched off. Make sure all windows and doors are securely locked — then relax after a job well done!!

12 Metrication

In this book both metric and Imperial weights and measures are given. The following tables show the comparisons.

Weights

The *basic* metric weight for foods is calculated in kilogrammes. One kilogramme is equivalent to 2.2lb (or nearly 2¼lb). Instead of ounces the metric measurement of weight is a gramme and in Britain we have accepted 25g as equivalent to 1oz. As the table below shows, there have to be adjustments from time to time, eg 6oz is 175g (not 6 x 25g = 150g). This is necessary to give a good result in the recipe.

ounces	actual grammes	accepted grammes	ounces	actual grammes	accepted grammes
1	28.35	25	9	255.15	250
2	56.7	50	10	283.5	275 or 300
3	85.05	75	11	311.85	300
4	113.4	100 or 110	12	340.2	350
5	141.75	125 or 150	13	368.55	375
6	170.1	175	14	396.90	400
7	198.45	200	15	425.25	425
8	226.8	225	16	453.60	450

Liquids

The BASIC measure for liquids is calculated in litres. One litre (1L) is equivalent to 1.76pts (or 1¾pt) or 35 fluid ounces (fl oz). The metric measure used for smaller quantities of liquid in Britain is a millilitre (ML); there are 1000 millilitres in 1 litre.

pints and fluid ounces	accurate litres and millilitres	accepted litres and millilitres	pints and fluid ounces	accurate litres and millilitres	accepted litres and millilitres
2 (40 fl oz)	1.136L or 1136ML	nearly 1¼L or 1200ML	½ (10 fl oz)	0.284L or 284ML	good¼L or 300ML
1 (20 fl oz)	0.568L or 568ML	good ½L or 600ML	¼ (5 fl oz)	0.142L or 142ML	good ⅛L or 150ML
¾ (15 fl oz)	0.426L or 426ML	scant ½L or 450ML	1 fl oz	0.0246L or 24.6ML	25ML

Length

The metric measurement of length is a metre, and most cooking utensils will be marked in centimetres (cm).

inches	actual centimetres	accepted centimetres	inches	actual centimetres	accepted centimetres
1	2.54	2.5	7	17.78	18.0
2	5.08	5.0	8	20.32	20.0
3	7.62	8.0	9	22.86	23.0
4	10.16	10.0	10	25.40	25.0
5	12.70	13.0	11	27.94	28.0
6	15.24	15.0	12	30.48	30.5

NB 'Tbspn' refers to a 15ml tablespoon and 'tspn' to a 5ml teaspoon.

Oven Temperatures

In Britain modern electric cookers have the degrees marked in Celsius (°C), rather than Fahrenheit (°F) as in the past. The tables give both °C and °F.

The comparative correct °C may be an awkward number, so the authorities have 'rounded this off'. Therefore the accurate Celsius degrees are given with the usual electric cooker setting in brackets.

The range of settings follows the oven descriptions.

A very cool oven:
93°C (90°C), 200°F, Gas Mark 0
107°C (110°C), 225°F, Gas Mark ¼
121°C (120°C), 250°F, Gas Mark ½

A low or cool oven:
135°C (140°C), 275°F, Gas Mark 1
149°C (150°C), 300°F, Gas Mark 2

I use the term 'very moderate' for the following setting, but in some manufacturers' books this is given as 'moderate':
163°C (160°C), 325°F, Gas Mark 3

Moderate:
177°C (180°C), 350°F, Gas Mark 4
190°C (190°C), 375°F, Gas Mark 5
(occasionally the latter temperature is given as 'moderately hot')

Moderately hot:
204°C (200°C), 400°F, Gas Mark 6

Hot:
218°C (220°C), 425°F, Gas Mark 7

Very hot:
232°C (230°C), 450°F, Gas Mark 8
246°C (240°C), 475°F, Gas Mark 9

Index